A Short History of
San Francisco

To my friend Jeff Werner
and my wife Laura Ferguson

... and I am following more than custom when I say
that without Charles Becker Sr. this book never would have been
written. To him my life-long gratitude. In addition, my thanks
and love to Alan Magary, Peter Dreyer, Craig Bergquist,
Christine Dunham, Gail Larrick, Bob Briggs, Elyce Wakerman,
Andrew Apter, Marjorie Ferguson, and Jeremiah Abrams.

A Short History of San Francisco

Tom Cole

A Monte Rosa Book

LEXIKOS

San Francisco

First published in May 1981 by
LEXIKOS
703 Market Street
San Francisco, California 94103

Designed in San Francisco by Craig Bergquist.
Text set in Stempel Palatino with Aster on
Mergenthaler Linoterm by Turner, Brown &
Yeoman, Inc. Graphic production by CABA
Design Office. Printed on Warren Olde Style
paper by Dharma Press, Oakland, California.

Manufactured in the United States of America

Library of Congress Cataloging in Publication
Data

Cole, Tom, 1947–
   A short history of San Francisco.

   "A Monte Rosa Book."
   Bibliography: p.
   Includes index.
   1. San Francisco (Calif.)—History.   I. Title.
   F869.S357C64   979.4'61   81-2588
   ISBN 0-938530-00-3 (pbk.)   AACR2
   ISBN 0-938530-01-1 (hbk.)

81 82 83 84 85 10 9 8 7 6 5 4 3 2 1

Contents

The Age of Innocence

1

From the top of a San Francisco hill, from a boat in the Bay, on a map or in memory, San Francisco Bay and its lands seem changeless. The hills are solid and the shore appears permanently etched. But what we call the Bay Area is permanent only to our scurrying human senses. In geologic time it is not much more than a sandbar on a beach, shifting, disappearing, forever being built and destroyed.

The full geological history of the Bay Area is impossible to know, and what is known is numbingly complex. The land has risen and fallen many times, the sea has invaded and retreated. It has been the bottom of a vast ocean and the marshy foraging ground of long-extinct creatures. But what of today's landscape, however fleeting scientists tell us it is?

The hills and waters and beaches of the Bay Area are the result of three natural forces, all of them, whether waxing or waning, still potent and active.

First was the eroding force of the Sacramento River, flowing south from its source near Mount Shasta, close to the Oregon border. Over the millennia the Sacramento has coursed over 250 miles down the flat Central Valley, ennobled along its route by run-off water from the countless streams and rivers that drain the western rampart of the Sierra Nevada. Today the mouth of the Sacramento is the Carquinez Strait, in the far northeast part of the Bay. But most scientists believe that during the Pleistocene Epoch, some 2.5 million years ago, the Sacramento flowed south and westward from the Carquinez, eroding a valley that is now the Bay. It kept flowing, theory has it, through what is now the Golden Gate, and met the ocean a few miles to the west of the present shoreline of the Pacific.

The Sacramento River's land-shaping was aided by the slow uplifting of the Coast Range, the second great force in the creation of the Bay. The Coast

Opposite page
The city to be: An 1830s watercolor, one of the earliest views ever made, shows the future dream city in its infancy.

Range is a relatively low but dramatic mountain chain that confronts the sea along most of the California coast. As it rose, the Coast Range blocked all the waters of Northern California from the sea—all, that is, except the Sacramento River, which kept its channel at the Golden Gate open. The mountains were forced up by shifting faults, deep cracks in California's unstable land. Those faults not only pushed up the Coast Range, but also buckled the land from north and south, deepening and defining the Sacramento's valley.

Then came the third and final force in the formation of the Bay. The end—some think it might just be a pause—of the most recent Ice Age began about 25,000 years ago. More than half of the earth's ice has melted since then, and, as sea level gradually rose, the ocean infiltrated the old valley and created San Francisco Bay.

The three major bay-building forces are still at work, subtly so in the case of the mysterious variations in climate that begin and end ice ages. The drought of 1976–77, the most severe this century in California, gave San Franciscans a lesson in the importance to the city, the state, and, in fact, the whole west, of those trends. The Sacramento River, backed up to the Carquinez by the ocean, is an important influence on the Bay's ecological health, and the valley canyons the Sacramento carved thousands of years ago have become shipping channels.

But the most troubling geological reality for the Bay Area is its restless land. Like all of California, the region is streaked with faults, the most famous and deadly of which, the San Andreas, caused the earthquake (and helped cause the fire) that almost destroyed San Francisco in 1906. The San Andreas doesn't touch San Francisco: it slithers into the ocean just south of the city and rejoins the mainland in Marin County, across the Golden Gate. There its path can be seen at narrow Tomales Bay, which was created by one of the fault's innumerable lurches. The San Andreas is just one of many faults—like the Hayward, which runs along the Berkeley Hills across the Bay from San Francisco—that constantly menace the Bay Area.

A Desolate Sandy Peninsula: The Bay's waters stopped rising about four or five thousand years ago. The hills had long been forested and, without all the paraphernalia of modern times, the Bay Area looked much the same as it does today. There weren't any eucalyptus groves—those came thousands of years later from Australia. And Alcatraz Island was still the nesting place of the pelicans for which it was named. But the meadow-dappled hills were that soothing mix of browns and

The Sacramento River contributes to the astounding quantity of water—seven times that of the Mississippi River at its mouth—that rushes through the Golden Gate daily.

Prehistoric San Francisco Bay was shallow—less than thirty feet deep over 85 percent of its area; since the Gold Rush, an amazing 40 percent of it has been reclaimed.

greens we know today. The waters changed mood and color endlessly, and elegant Mount Tamalpais watched over the land. Amidst all that beauty—almost surrounded by it—was a peninsula, the thumb of a cupped hand, and, at the tip of that peninsula, the less than fifty square miles we now call San Francisco.

The ancestral San Francisco Peninsula was a counterpoint to the lushness around it. There were few trees and fewer meadows, and little of the wildlife that teemed elsewhere. It was—except for a few patches of verdure—a desolate and windy place. But most striking was the blanket of sand under which the site of today's city was buried, sand eroded from the cliffs to the south, carried by local currents to San Francisco's long beach, and from there blown across the upper peninsula by persistent westerly winds.

For ages the sand piled up: the longest sand dunes on the Pacific Coast stretched from Ocean Beach to—at one point near the anchorage of the Bay Bridge—the Bay itself, a distance of more than six miles. Sand drifts crested 600-foot Golden Gate Heights and covered much of Mount Sutro's 900 feet. City Hall, five miles from the ocean, is built on 80 feet of the stuff. In fact, much of the relatively flat Sunset and Richmond Districts in the western part of the city would be as hilly as the rest of San Francisco were their contours not buried by sand.

The westerly winds which create surf on the Pacific coast blow across the continent and flatten surf on the Atlantic coast; they would still be at work burying the city in sand if it weren't for the windbreak created when Golden Gate Park was built in the 1870s.

A **Doomed Race:** The Ohlone Indians were the first humans to settle around the Bay. They were part of the Pleistocene Epoch migration of Asian peoples across the land bridge that is now the Bering Strait. About four or five thousand years ago, the Ohlone ended their age-long trek and made their home on the Bay's shores.

When the Ohlone found the great Bay, it was still being filled. We know, or suspect this, because a few feet of some of the shell mounds the Indians left are below sea level: they were begun—the first of thousands of layers of shells, the residue of thousands of feasts—when the Bay's waters were rising.

These shell mounds, cut, quartered, and dissected by generations of archaeologists and anthropologists, are a revealing signature of the Ohlone way of life. Over 400 mounds have been found on the shores of the Bay, some as much as 30 feet high, 600 feet long, and 200 feet wide. Anthropologists have long known—they have massive evidence—that the Ohlone had a taste for shellfish. Around the turn of the century, however, a scientist named N. C. Nelson listed some of the other animal remains he had found in the mounds.

The Age of Innocence

Nelson's catalogue opens our eyes to the marvelous variety of wildlife in and around the prehistoric Bay. He identified the bones of deer, elks, sea otters, beavers, squirrels, rabbits, gophers, raccoons, badgers, skunks, wildcats, dogs, seals, sea lions, porpoises, whales, canvasback ducks, geese, cormorants, "waders, or some large birds," turtles, "skates, thornbacks and other fish," wolves, and grizzly bears.

In addition to this wealth of animal life, the Ohlone ate acorn meal and acorn bread as a staple (an early Spanish explorer called the bread "deliciously rich and oily.") The Ohlone were free from civilized daintiness and there was little they didn't eat; included in their diet were insects, animal entrails, and all kinds of seeds and roots. To the Spanish, the Ohlone diet was bestial. Seeing them digging for roots and the reeds used in basket making, the Spanish gave them the name "diggers," by which they were vulgarly known as long as they existed.

The more polite Spaniards called the local Indians Costanoans, as have most anthropologists. Today, Ohlone—obscure in origin, but at least an Indian word—seems preferable.

As easy as it was for the Spanish (who called almost all Indians diggers) to pigeonhole them, the Ohlone had little sense of nationhood. "Tribes did not exist in California in the sense in which the word is . . . applicable to the greater part of the North American Continent," wrote the pioneering anthropologist A. L. Kroeber in 1922. What we call the Ohlone, Yurok, or Hupa "tribe" was actually an ethnic group rather than a political entity. The 10,000 or so Ohlone who inhabited coastal California from the Bay to Point Sur (100 miles to the south) were split up into about forty "tribelets," each with its own closely held identity, many with a unique language.

The tribelets were presided over by a chief, but his (occasionally her) authority was that of an exemplar of tribal virtues. As Malcom Margolin puts it in his evocative book *The Ohlone Way*, "The chief was not seen as someone who would energetically lead the people to a new or better way of life." The Ohlone, to the mystification of the Spanish, the Mexicans, and the settlers from the United States who poured in during the 1840s, had no desire to better their lot. Instead, they were dedicated to maintaining as changeless a way of life as possible.

The Ohlone lived steadfastly and, it seems, happily in the "here and now." The past was barely acknowledged: to use a dead person's name was indecent, to dream about the deceased called for a visit to the tribal shaman. As Kroeber wrote, "No one knew his own age nor how remote an event was that happened more than a dozen years ago. . . . Most groups had not even a word for 'year' but employed 'world,' 'summer,' or 'winter' instead."

The Ohlone were successful in their insistence on sticking with a good thing. Nelson proved that by picking his way through every level of the shell mounds and finding "no form of artifact . . . at the bottom of the accumulations that does not also occur at the top." As hunter-gatherers, the Ohlone had little need to invent new implements. The bows and arrows, mortars and pestles of the earliest Indians served the last, and the hundreds of generations in between, admirably. But the Ohlone were more than passive guests of the land. They practiced remarkably scientific land management. By selective burning, they insured a steady supply of their favorite grasses, made pasturage available to their game animals, and prevented the buildup of combustible materials. As Malcom Margolin puts it, "The Ohlone did not practice agriculture or develop a rich material culture, not because they failed but because they succeeded so well in the most ancient of all ways of life." The land was simply too rich and the climate too favorable to force the Ohlone to innovate and develop new strategies for existence.

Each tribelet was in a state of almost constant, elegantly paced migration: here to the hills for the acorn harvest, there to the marshes for water fowl (the Bay's skies were once filled with plump birds), then to the ocean for a visit to the ancestral shell mound, and back to the meadows and forests for elk and deer hunting. An Ohlone's life was one of movement, but the tribelet's territory was small, and a person would probably die within a few miles of where he or she was born. The Ohlone lived in reciprocal intimacy with the land. Each landmark—streams, boulders, an old, friendly oak tree—had a name, a deep resonance. Because they were so deeply rooted in their environment, and because their land and waters were so abundant, the Ohlone rarely warred; what wars they indulged in were highly ritualized and usually ended with the first casualty.

When the Spanish arrived, they found the Indians' distaste for wrestling with nature and each other proof that they were "*bestias.*" But an even worse sin than merry indolence and lack of high-powered civilization was what the Europeans wrongheadedly saw as an absence of religion in Ohlone life.

Religion to the Spanish and religion to the Ohlone were very different things. For the Spaniard, religion had to do with churches, ceremonies and hierarchies, and above all an often frantic belief in the consolation of life after death. But the Ohlone lived in a great natural cathedral and didn't much seek the solace of an afterlife. In any case, their lives were filled with sometimes subtle, sometimes rambunctious ceremony. Almost every act, especially those involving hunting and food gathering, was connected to a public or private ritual. To the Ohlone, as to most primitive people, religion and daily life were one and the same. That the Spanish were unable to see or appreciate this was tragic. Their basic misunderstanding of Ohlone culture fueled the contempt that led them to destroy the Ohlone.

A. Golden Gate
B. Sacramento River
C. Carquinez Straits
D. San Andreas Fault
E. Drake's Bay
F. Point Sur

The Age of Innocence

Nova Albion: In 1579 Francis Drake—later knighted, but at the time a royally sanctioned pirate and explorer—became the first European to land on the shores of Northern California. For two and a half years, Drake had been looting Spanish ships and settlements in the West Indies and along the South American coast. By the time he reached California, only one of his five original ships, the celebrated *Golden Hind*, was left. Drake and his crew were weary and bedraggled and the *Golden Hind*, loaded down with bounty and survivors, was badly in need of repair. In June Drake landed his ship somewhere in what is now Marin County.

The exact location of Drake's landfall is the subject of a long and cherished debate. Some argue that the *Golden Hind* entered San Francisco Bay itself and anchored at a spot near today's infamous San Quentin prison. But most think that a master sailor like Drake would have had more to say about one of the world's great natural anchorages than merely to call it "a convinient and fit harborough." So it seems that Drake missed the entrance to the Bay (June is a foggy month) and landed on the Marin shore to the north, perhaps at Bodega Bay, Bolinas Bay, or Point Reyes, but most likely at the eponymous Drake's Bay on Point Reyes Peninsula, about twenty-five miles northwest of San Francisco.

The mystery of Drake's landfall is complicated by the "Plate of Brasse" which, according to the voyage's chaplain and chronicler, Francis Fletcher, Drake left behind. The plate, Fletcher wrote, commemorated the landing, named the newly discovered land "Nova Albion," and claimed it for "Queen Elizabeth and Herr Successors Forever." Such a plate—another curlicue in an already baroque controversy—was found in 1936 near San Quentin, of all places. How did the plate get there from Drake's Bay? Or did Drake really land at San Quentin? In any case, the plate rests today in the University of California's Bancroft Library, where over the years countless bunkers and debunkers have peered at it. The latter seem to have carried the day, though, and most authorities now consider the plate an ingenious and anonymous forgery. (But not all agree, and the debate goes on. . . .)

Drake and his crew spent a comfortable six weeks at wherever it was they landed. The Englishmen repaired the *Golden Hind* and built a small fort (an undiscovered archaeological treasure, even if only a few stones or planks remain. The local Indians, probably Coast Miwoks, visited the intruders and, as was their custom, brought gifts and friendliness.

With the *Golden Hind* reprovisioned and once again seaworthy, Drake and his crew set out from Nova Albion to continue their historic circumnavigation of the world. Almost two hundred years passed before the peace of Northern California's land and waters was again disturbed by outsiders.

A Short History of San Francisco

Enter the Spanish: When Drake made his hazy claim to Nova Albion, the Spanish were already firmly established in Central and South America and Baja (or lower) California. Since Juan Cabrillo's expedition in 1542, they had also claimed Alta California, the land north of Mexico—though they had little idea what they were claiming.

The Spanish were worried and intrigued by Drake's claim. Nova Albion seemed to them a part of their mysterious Alta California. Though the Spanish Empire was already tottery and overextended, it very slowly began to take an interest in the lands north of Mexico. For not only were the English casting about for new domains, the French and Russians were too. As a Russian visitor to California put it as late as 1816, "With an avariciousness of spirit, Spain extends her territory here, merely because she envies the others the room."

Luckily for Spain, none of her rivals proved very competitive. For almost two centuries, the Spanish dallied before planting their flag in what is now California. But in the end it was more than simple jealousy or greed that motivated the empire. As difficult as it was to colonize and exploit, Alta California already had one crop sown and ready to be harvested: the pagan souls of the Indians.

Spanish missionaries of the Franciscan order had been in the New World since Columbus's second voyage in 1493. By the late 1760s, the Franciscans were eager to begin the spiritual conquest of Alta California. The head of the Franciscans in California was Father Junípero Serra, a slight, chronically ill, but religiously impassioned man. Serra had a fiery desire to bring the Indians into the True Faith, and it was he and his fellows who were the prime movers of the long-delayed Spanish push into Alta California.

In May 1769, Father Serra and Gaspar de Portolá, a Spanish nobleman and the first governor of the Californias, led a so-called Sacred Expedition north from Sonora, Mexico. After a grueling overland march in the summer heat, the expedition reached San Diego (the beginning of Alta California) in late June. The expedition included three ships and one other overland group. Three hundred men set out for Alta California. Only about half of them ever arrived.

On July 16, Father Serra founded the Mission of San Diego de Alcalá, the first of the twenty-one missions the Franciscans would build in California. The missionaries immediately set about saving the Indian soul. In practice, this meant herding as many natives as possible into the missions where they could be taught to act . . . correctly.

From San Diego, Portolá continued northward toward Monterey Bay,

The Age of Innocence

which had been discovered in 1602 by Sebastián Vizcaíno. The latter's descriptions had been enticing, and in the 167 years since Vizcaíno's discovery, Monterey (less than 100 miles south of San Francisco Bay, but almost 400 miles north of San Diego) had become something of an obsession for the Spanish. For three months, Portolá's party struggled through the hot, dry hill country of California in search of the beautiful and by now almost mythical Monterey.

But Vizcaíno had seen the bay from the sea, after all, and in the end Portolá's expedition utterly failed to recognize Monterey. On November 1, 1769 Portolá sent a scouting group north. Sgt. José Ortega's band worked its way up the shoreline of the Peninsula, along present-day Ocean Beach, past today's Cliff House, and up to the tip of the Peninsula, where they gazed with some surprise across the grand strait of the Golden Gate and into the immense Bay itself.

But Ortega and his men were foot soldiers, and the significance of discovering a harbor into which—as more than one visitor was to write—"all the navies of the world might fit" seems to have escaped them. In any case, the expedition was under orders to find Monterey. As Portolá later wrote his superiors, "Under all circumstances I shall always give preference to the Port of Monterey in order not to depart a jot from my blind and resigned obedience." When Ortega's scouting group returned to Portolá, they brought bad news: since the way north was blocked (by a bay much superior to Monterey's), further exploration was impractical. The obedient Portolá led his expedition back to San Diego.

The next year, Portolá was finally able to locate Monterey Bay. Father Serra dedicated his second mission, and a few miles away the soldiers, following Spanish imperial practice (modeled after that of the Romans), built a military outpost, the Monterey Presidio.

Perhaps because of all the energy that had gone into finding it, Monterey was always the cynosure of Spanish power in Alta California. But once Monterey was accounted for, the huge Bay to the north could at last be explored. Pedro Fages, who became governor when Portolá left California in 1770, led two expeditions to San Francisco and succeeded in mapping all but the Bay's northern reaches. By this time, Spain had little expansionist energy left, and what remained was often diluted by political bickering and bureaucratic punctilio. And, too, the journey from Baja California to Monterey and San Francisco by land or sea (where the currents were adverse) was long and difficult. It was apparent that Alta California was an inviting and ripe land, both in Indian souls and natural promise. But it was spectacularly distant from Spain, and not effectively much closer to Mexico City.

The name San Francisco, first for the harbor, later for the mission and the city, came about through a geographical mix-up. In 1595 Sebastián Cermeño had landed at Drake's Bay and (re)named it for the founder of the Franciscan order. (Like Drake, he missed the larger harbor a few miles to the south.) Even before Portolá finally reached Monterey, Father Serra had plans to found a mission "on the port of Our Father, San Francisco." When the Bay was at last discovered, it was confused with Cermeño's (or Drake's) bay and given that bay's Spanish name.

A Short History of San Francisco

The Mission and the Ohlone: In 1775 the decision was finally made to establish permanent outposts by the Bay of San Francisco. In late September a group of 250 soldiers and colonists led by Captain Juan Bautista de Anza set out from northern Mexico. One thousand five hundred miles and nearly six months later, the heroic band arrived at Monterey. De Anza then selected fourteen especially hardy trekkers and set out for the Bay.

At eight in the morning of March 28, 1776, the Spaniards reached the sandy tip of the Peninsula. De Anza had a cross erected to mark a site for a presidio, "on the extreme point of the white cliff at the inner terminus of the mouth of the port"—today's Fort Point. It was a beautiful and historic morning. Father Pedro Font, who blessed the cross, wrote in his diary that if the site "could be well settled like Europe there would not be anything more beautiful in the world."

A. Ohlone territory
B. Sacramento River
C. San Diego
D. Camino Real

The next day, the expedition put up a second cross three miles to the southeast, next to a small stream on the relatively lush lee side of the Peninsula. This was to be the location of the sixth California mission, named—as Father Serra had planned years before—for the gentle founder of the Franciscan order, Saint Francis of Assisi. Three months passed before the lonely group of soldiers and missionaries camped on the Peninsula received permission from Monterey to begin building permanent settlements. And another three months went by before the arrival of the packet *San Carlos*, the first ship (if the *Golden Hind*'s claim is discounted) to enter the Bay. The *San Carlos* brought essential men and supplies, and on September 17, 1776, the first building of the Presidio was completed. Three weeks later, the mission was formally dedicated.

The Ohlone and the other tribes of the Bay, the Miwoks, the Carquin, and the Santa Clara, had greeted the Spanish with their customary grace. Captain Don Manuel de Ayala of the *San Carlos* wrote in his official report that, "The best [of San Francisco Bay's many advantages] is that the heathen Indians around this port are so constant in their good friendship and so gentle in their manners." To the Indians, the Spanish, with their baubles and beads, mirrors and guns, must have seemed miraculous apparitions. After all, these were people who had lived for thousands of years using the same time-honored and tested artifacts.

The missionaries were intent upon rescuing the indigenes from their innocence. So, with promises of further material and spiritual miracles, they lured the Indians to the missions, baptized them, and installed them as chattels of the Church. At the Mission of Saint Francis, as in all the missions, the tribelets and tribes were randomly mixed. The crucial, carefully

The Presidio is still an active army base, which can—and does—boast that it was "Founded in 1776." But all that remains of San Francisco's oldest building is part of a wall incorporated into the base's Officers' Club. The mission became known as the Mission Dolores after the long-gone lake, Laguna de los Dolores, next to which it was built. It was rebuilt in 1791 and, notwithstanding the myriad of Spanish-named streets, remains San Francisco's only compelling link with its colonial past.

The Age of Innocence

maintained differences between Indian groups were irrelevant to the priests. The Indians were crowded into barracks and set to work gardening, cloth weaving, and becoming civilized.

Otto von Kotzebue, the German-born captain of the Russian exploring ship *Rurik*, who visited San Francisco Bay in 1816, wrote of the degradation of the Indians in his book *A Voyage of Discovery* (1821), "The uncleanliness of these barracks baffles description and is perhaps the cause of the great mortality, for of 1,000 Indians at San Francisco, 300 die each year. The Indian girls, of whom 400 live in the Mission, live separate from the men, likewise in such barracks; both sexes are obliged to labor hard."

They were allowed a few traditional pastimes such as gambling and dancing, but their once free lives were chiefly taken up by their dull tasks. They listened to the Mass—always said in incomprehensible Latin—and they learned the prayers taught them by the priests. Von Kotzebue wrote of the "contempt" the missionaries had for the Indians: "None of [the priests] appear to have troubled themselves about [Indian] history, customs, religions or languages."

Perhaps the saddest act in this tragedy was the forced removal of the Indians from the land that had nurtured them for so many centuries. Von Kotzebue wrote movingly of the short reprieves from mission life the Indians were allowed:

> Twice in a year they receive permission to return to their homes. This short time is the happiest period of their existence, and I myself have seen them going home in crowds with loud rejoicings. The sick, who cannot undertake the journey, at least accompany their happy countrymen to the shore where they embark, and there sit for days, together mournfully gazing on the distant summits of the mountains which surround their homes. They often sit in this posture for several days, without taking any food, so much does the sight of their lost home affect these new Christians. Every time, some of those who have permission run away; and they would probably all do it, were they not deterred by their fear of the soldiers, who catch them and bring them back to the Mission as criminals.

The Colonial Era: Chasing down escaped Indians was one of the few breaks in the stale life of the Presidio's soldiers, stuck out on the teemless Peninsula north of the Mission. Some of them might have found solace in the stupendous view, and the occcasional bear-bull fight was always a festive occasion. But the soldiers and their Presidio were neglected from the beginning. In 1792 the English explorer George Vancouver described the already run-down "fort." He noticed a single cannon, "lashed to a rotten carriage." In fact, the Presidio was so inconspicuous that Vancouver missed it and anchored instead at Yerba Buena Cove on the upper northeast part of the Peninsula. The cove, named for the "good herb" that flourished there, was to become the setting for the pueblo that grew into San Francisco.

Twenty-four years after Vancouver's visit, the *Rurik's* naturalist Adelbert von Chamisso noted that the Presidio officers complained "of the misery in which they languished, forgotten and deserted [and unpaid] for six or seven years." The Presidio depended on the Mission for its food, and the priests "would deliver nothing to them without a requisition, and even then only that which was hardly indispensible to their sustenence, this not including bread or meal."

In 1821 Mexico took advantage of Spain's weakness and declared its independence, first as an empire, then in 1824 as a republic. Mexico naturally considered Alta California part of its property. But the new nation had more pressing concerns than its remote northern outposts, and the Mission and Presidio were left to their own devices.

Twelve years after independence, the Mexican government passed a Secularization Act, stripping the once feudal missions of almost all their land. The Indians, too, were "secularized," but by this time they had little to gain from freedom. A return to tribal life was impossible, and the Indians—those few who remained after disease and despair had taken their toll—drifted into the few small pueblos of Alta California, or became semislaves on the cattle ranches springing up in the interior.

Though Mexico lacked the means to exploit its northern colonies, it encouraged settlement by issuing generous land grants. Colonists who took advantage of those grants found California's warm inland valleys well suited to cattle raising. Within a decade of Mexican independence, a lively hide and tallow trade had grown up between the ranches and ships in San Francisco Bay. Whalers in search of reprovisioning also called, and word of the Bay and the fertile (and underpopulated) land around it began to spread.

In 1816 the Russians, tantalized by von Kotzebue's descriptions, had already established a trade and sealing base at Fort Ross, sixty miles north of the Bay. The French had explored California in 1786 and were, as usual, looking for new colonies. And, of course, the English were never ones to forget a land-claim, however ancient.

But—to the Mexicans at least—the most troublesome coveter of Alta California was the feisty nation to the east—the United States of America. In

No *yerba buena* grows amid the concrete and glass of the financial district that now occupies the site of the old cove, but the visitor can see and smell *Satureja douglasii* (the scientific name of the Spaniards' "good herb") in the Garden of Fragrance in Golden Gate Park's Strybing Arboretum.

George Vancouver insisted on calling the area around San Francisco Bay "New Albion" when he visited it in the 1790s—a sign of England's continued interest in Drake's two-century-old claim.

1835 President Andrew Jackson had offered Mexico $500,000 for San Francisco Bay. And when Texas broke away from Mexico in 1836 (and soon joined the Union), a disturbing precedent for American expansion had been set.

Official America might have been looking across the continent, but to the average American in the 1830s, Alta California was somewhere behind the back of the beyond. But there were a few plucky folks from "The States" who found their way to Alta California, one of whom, an ex-Harvard student named Richard Henry Dana, did much to put the obscure land on the map.

Dana had left Harvard in 1834, after a serious illness, and had signed on aboard a ship bound for the Pacific and the hide and tallow trade in San Francisco Bay. When he sailed into the Bay in 1835, the Presidio was all but deserted and the decaying Mission without the services of a full-time priest. But Dana was a forward-looking fellow. In his book *Two Years Before the Mast* (published in 1840) he depicted the magnificient Bay, with its "large and beautifully wooded islands . . . the abundance of water, the extreme fertility of its shores; the excellence of its climate, which is as near being perfect as any in the world [though "for three weeks it rained almost every hour, without cessation"], its facilities for navigation affording the best anchorage-grounds on the whole western coast of America,—all fit for a place of great importance." Indeed, he wrote with delightful prescience, "If California ever becomes a prosperous country this bay will be the center of its prosperity."

By the time of Dana's visit, trade had already increased to the point where ship chandlers and middlemen were becoming needed. The center of the Bay Area's—if not yet California's—prosperity was the soggy little harbor of Yerba Buena, the natural anchorage for trading ships in the Bay.

The first enterprising gent to set up business by the Bay was an English whaling captain named William Richardson. In 1822 Richardson had left the ship *Orion* and settled by the Bay. He married María Martínez, the Presidio *comandante*'s daughter, and, following politic custom, became a Mexican citizen and Catholic convert. After a few years in the southern part of the province, Richardson returned to Yerba Buena, and in 1835 built the first civilian habitation—"a shanty of rough boards," Dana called it—to grace the shores of San Francisco Bay. Two years later, busily engaged in ferrying goods around the Bay, Richardson built a second house, a two-storied adobe called the Casa Grande. Richardson's house occupied what is now 827–43 Grant Avenue (between Washington and Clay Streets in the heart of Chinatown). Then called the Calle de la Fundación, Grant is San Francisco's oldest street.

William Richardson bought two schooners which the missionaries had acquired from the Russians at Fort Ross, a settlement founded in 1812. In 1841 Fort Ross (the restored remains of which can be seen today just off Highway 1) was abandoned by the Russians because of dwindling fur supplies and the distant threat of the Monroe Doctrine, which promised to exclude foreign settlements from the continent.

A Short History of San Francisco

Tiny Yerba Buena was beginning to grow. Jacob Leese secured a small land grant in 1836 and built the village's third house, across the street from the Casa Grande. Leese's wife Rosalia (the sister of General Mariano Vallejo, head of Alta California's most prominent family) soon gave birth to the new town's first baby, a girl, who was given her mother's name.

In the 1850s, when San Francisco was exploding in size and importance, an early settler named Joseph Downey, using the pseudonym "The Old Saw," wrote about Yerba Buena as it had been in its infancy. He described for his Gold Rush readers—to whom the quiet village must have seemed an ancient myth—the house that was "rum shop, bakery, grocery, and dwelling place for a jolly lot of Dutchmen who rusticated there," the wooden frame building, a "bad imitation of [a] New England cottage," where lived the "big gun of the village—the major domo—Señor Don José Jesus de Noé, as fair, full and radiant specimen of beef-fed Californian as was ever put on exhibition."

In 1845 Yerba Buena was an alternately dusty and windblown, shabby kind of place, inhabited by a couple of hundred people—Americans, Indians, Spanish, Dutch, and a few Kanakas from the Sandwich Isles. The

Yerba Buena Cove in late 1848: Waves lapped at what is now the middle of San Francisco's Financial District. Plaques at the corners of Market and First and Bush and Market streets mark the original shoreline of Yerba Buena Cove.

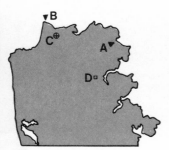

A. Yerba Buena
B. Fort Point
C. Presidio
D. Mission Dolores

inhabitants, "The Old Saw" remembered, "one and all lived and loved together, and their eternal routine of drinking, smoking and dancing was never interrupted save by an occasional rodeo kicked up by the wild boys of the ranches, the periodical visitations of hide droggers, or the rare appearance of a man-of-war, or whale ship in the harbor." It was the hide and tallow trade, above all, that kept them in drink and smoke:

> Upon the arrival of one of the ships the California telegraph (a fast horse) soon spread the news far and near, and for days and weeks the port was crowded with the sturdy rancheros and their dark-eyed senioritas, rushing to purchase such goods as most pleased the fancy and suited their wants. The articles brought for sale were retained on board the ships, which were fitted up expressly for trade and each had a large storeroom on the between decks, where the stocks were displayed... No credit was asked or expected, but all bills were settled... by a draft... paid in bank notes (i.e.) hides, horns and tallow minted from the backs and bodies of the thousands of cattle which swarmed in every valley of the country.

Yerba Buena was already a small sample of what it would become: a polyglot congregation of hustlers, vagabonds, eccentrics, hedonists, and traders—above all, traders. But in the cattle ranches around the Bay another, much more couth society held sway.

Rancheros and Yankees: For a few years a benign pastoral peace reigned in Alta California. "The Splendid Idle Forties," as novelist Gertrude Atherton later called them, were presided over by the Spanish-Mexican rancheros, temporary heirs of a splendid land. They enjoyed a carefree way of life and created a society molded to hearty pleasure. The caballeros—freed from undue labor by their Indian serfs—cultivated the manly arts: riding, roping, and hunting. The women, "in many ways like grown-up children," as one of them later wrote, devoted themselves to "dancing, music, religion and amiability."

Later in the century, Guadalupe Vallejo, General Vallejo's nephew, remembered that in the 1840s "fewer than fifty Spanish families [lived] in the region about San Francisco Bay, and they were closely connected by ties of blood or intermarriage." Theirs was a society in which Spanish blood was admired, and families boasted of having "come with Portolá." But the rancheros and their kin—some of whose names, such as Moraga, Vallejo, Martinez, and Livermore (like Richardson, a sea captain), were given to towns in the Bay Area—were a kindly, if snobbish, lot.

In the old Spanish tradition, they cultivated the arts of hospitality. In 1949 a writer named Julia Cooley Altrocchi wrote of early California in her book *Spectacular San Franciscans*. Altrocchi was a wistful admirer of the "joyous, beautiful" Spanish life that moved "like a carousel all around the prosaic American settlement [Yerba Buena]." She contrasted the Spanish and Yankee styles in a parable of what was to happen to the Spanish-Mexican culture: "When the Yankees came in, and the courteous Spaniard greeted him at the door with: *'La casa es suya'* ('the house is yours,' implying everything in it is at your disposal) the Yankee took him literally and seized everything in sight." Before the Yankees arrived in force, Guadalupe Vallejo remembered, "There was never a more peaceful or happy people on the face of the earth than the Spanish, Mexican and Indian population of Alta California."

But the joyous carousel ride was short. Alta California was too tempting—its soil too fertile, its climate too pleasant, its harbor at San Francisco too commodious and handy—to remain in the hands of landed aristocrats. Word of the region's charms had been spreading east, carried by Dana, and by adventurers, trappers, and sailors. By the early 1840s, an ever-increasing trickle of Yankee migration to California was under way.

A trapper named Ribideaux inflamed the wanderlust of young John Bidwell of Kansas, who wrote that the frontiersman said "there was but one man in California that had a chill . . . and it was a matter of such wonderment to the people of Monterey that they went eighteen miles into the country to see him shake." In May 1841 Bidwell gathered a brave company and began the mysterious trek from the Mississippi to California. Six months later, Bidwell's band—"The first that went direct to California from the East," he said—reached their promised land. Bidwell estimated there were fewer than 100 foreigners in California.

There were soon more. Alfred Robinson, who had been in California since 1829, wrote in 1846, "In this age of 'annexation' why not extend the 'area of freedom' by the annexation of California." Like Dana, Robinson saw San Francisco Bay as the natural center of the rich land, "San Francisco . . . is the point," he wrote, "why not plant the banner of liberty there?"

The American settlers of the 1840s were of a different sort than Don William Antonio Richardson or Jacob Leese, who enjoyed offering hospitality as much as any of his trans-Bay neighbors. For one thing, the immigrants were beginning to come by land, across the vast western desert and over the Sierra Nevada, which had first been crossed by the legendary Jedediah Smith in 1827. It was a long and soul-trying journey, made worse in the earliest years by what Bidwell called "our [complete] ignorance of the route." Later such stalwarts as Captain John C. Frémont and his companion

Kit Carson explored the routes across the Sierra that made large-scale crossings feasible. But it was never easy. The tragedy of the Donner Party of 1847, which was trapped high in the mountains by early snows and resorted to cannibalism, is part of Western folklore.

More important than how the newcomers got there was what they brought with them. The earliest Americans in California had usually arrived with few worldly goods and, being in a minority, settled into the palmy Hispanic way of life, converted to Catholicism, married into a Mexican family, and became upstanding citizens of Mexico. But the new Yankee colonists often arrived with a wagonload of family and looked with narrowed eyes on Catholicism. For many of them, the "eternal routine of drinking, smoking and dancing," the silky ways of ranch life, were wasteful and decadent.

John Bidwell was an exception. He became a devotee of the Old California, and mirrored the wariness with which the new settlers were often greeted when he wrote, "They were not generally a class calculated to gain much favor with the people." To the Mexican Government, the Americans were not only a rather crude bunch, they were also a clear threat to Mexico's tenuous hold over Alta California. Many of them made no secret of wanting to "extend the area of freedom," and few had much reverence for Mexican law. When the trickle of incomers was becoming a torrent in the mid-1840s, Pio Pico, the fourteenth and last governor of Alta California, complained, "We find ourselves threatened by hordes of Yankee emigrants... whose progress we cannot arrest."

The coming annexation of California was so eagerly awaited that many were impatient to get it over with. As early as 1842, for instance, Commodore Thomas ap Catesby Jones had sailed into Monterey harbor and seized the town. Jones, not normally so impetuous, was under the impression that war between Mexico and the United States had been declared. Informed of his error, he apologized, handed back the town, and sailed off.

Mexico resisted the Yankee hordes by passing restrictive laws, ordering some of the rowdiest settlers to leave, and attempting to curtail trade. But those rough Yanks were the wave of the future, and Mexico's attempts at inhospitality served mainly to enrage them. As time passed, and the Mexican presence became ever more feeble, they were quite happy to be enraged anyway. Mexican "injustices" merely hurried the inevitable: it was increasingly evident that the Americans in California were soon going to be in a position to declare an independent republic, or that the United States government was simply going to grab California.

One of the Americans the Mexicans were eager to rid themselves of was the brilliant explorer and writer John Charles Frémont, a captain in the U.S. Army's Topographical Corps. With a contingent of 40 men, he had explored the Rocky Mountains in the early 1840s. They continued on to the Oregon Territory in 1843 before turning south to explore and investigate Alta California.

Exploration came naturally to Frémont, who was a tough and talented geographer. So, too, did the rabble-rousing he did in California. A blithe imperialist and a believer in America's manifest destiny in the West, he was also a cantankerous and willful man, who in later years got into many scrapes with his own government (he was court-martialed in 1847 for disobedience). But in the early and mid-1840s, Frémont was convinced that his ambitions coincided with those of his Washington superiors—namely, as he wrote, "to obtain possession of California." In 1845 Frémont published an account of his California explorations that did much to excite the United States to the region's potential. His "Report of the Exploring Expedition to Oregon and North California," also showed the extent of Mexico's weakness.

In 1846, egged on by his influential and expansionist father-in-law, Senator Thomas Hart Benton of Missouri, Frémont returned to California with an armed band of sixty men. He was soon expelled by the Mexicans and left for Oregon. Within a few weeks he had returned, however, and in little more than a month had helped to create the rebellious fervor that led to the almost mythical and rather comic Bear Flag Revolt.

As it happened, the war between land-rich Mexico and the militant United States had been going on for a month and two days when a clamjamfery of rebellious Americans stormed into General Mariano Vallejo's estate in Sonoma on June 14, 1846. There they announced the formation of a California Republic and, over numerous brandies offered by the polite general, sewed together a flag featuring a somewhat forlorn grizzly which was raised above Sonoma's plaza.

California legend portrays the Bear Flaggers as courageous revolutionaries, latter-day Tom Paines and George Washingtons. But historian and novelist Kevin Starr is probably closer to the mark in describing the revolt's leaders, six-foot, six-inch Robert B. Semple and William Ide, an aggressively naive man, who was the first and only president of the California Republic, as "perfect examples, near parodies in fact, of the liquor-inflamed frontier orator and the nasal Yankee crank." Which was which is beside the point—as was the revolt itself. For while Sonoma was dozing under the vinous rule of the California Republic, the rest of Alta California was quickly coming under U.S. control.

The village of Yerba Buena became part of "The States" on July 9, 1846, when seventy soldiers and marines from the ship *Portsmouth* (which had been lying handy in the Bay for some time) marched ashore and raised the American flag in the village's plaza. "The Old Saw," a marine himself at the time, described the epochal moment:

> To the soul-inspiring air of Yankee Doodle from our band, consisting of one
> drum and fife, with an occasional put in from a stray dog or disconsolate

It was Frémont who named the Golden Gate (*Chrysopylae*) on the analogy of Istanbul's Golden Horn (*Chrysoceras*). He predicted that the former would come to rival the latter in importance, and he was right.

Yerba Buena's plaza was promptly renamed Portsmouth Square in 1846, and for many years was the heart of San Francisco. Today, it is a pleasant, smallish park on the edge of Chinatown, somewhat overshadowed by the massive hotel across the street.

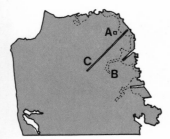

A. Portsmouth Square
B. Original shoreline
C. Market Street

jackass on the line of march, [we] trudged proudly up through Montgomery Street to Clay, up Clay to the plaza... Capt. M[ontgomery] had a proclamation all ready prepared and our first Lieutenant now read it to the assembled crowd and when he finished gave the signal, and in a moment, amid the roar of cannon from the ship, and hurrahs of the ship's company, the vivas of the Californians, the cheers of the Dutchmen, the barking of dogs, braying of jackasses and a general confusion of sounds from every living thing within hearing, that flag floated up, which has never been lowered to mortal foe.

There was some nervousness (the explosion of an exotic coffee-maker "caused the long roll to be beat, for the Spaniards had come to take the city"), but the takeover of Yerba Buena was pleasantly bloodless. The real war between Mexico and the United States didn't end until the treaty of Guadalupe Hidalgo was signed in early February 1848, but by that time Yerba Buena had long since become a tiny but promising part of the United States of America.

The Infant Colossus: The pueblo's population was more than doubled on July 31, when the ship *Brooklyn* arrived from New York after six months at sea. Aboard were 238 Mormons fleeing persecution and moral corruption. The newcomers had expected to meet up in California with Brigham Young and the main group of Latter-Day Saints. But Young had stopped his hegira at the Great Salt Lake in Utah. One of the *Brooklyn*'s passengers, 20-year-old E. C. Kemble, later described the Mormons' disappointment. Not only were their coreligionists absent, but "Instead of the soft airs of the Italian clime which Frémont, [Lansford] Hastings and other writers had described," the Mormons had found themselves "on bleak, treeless and apparently verdureless shores... a cold wind swept around... and a grey fog distilled dampness and shrouded the landscape in gloom."

Kemble was an early critic of San Francisco's summer climate. The classic comment is "The coldest winter I ever spent was a summer in San Francisco," attributed to Mark Twain. But then again, San Francisco enjoys its balmiest days in September and October, when most other places are getting ready for winter.

It wasn't only the weather that displeased the Saints of Nauvoo. They had expected to land in Zion, not the United States. Their elder, an energetic and quick-witted 26-year-old named Sam Brannan, saw the Stars and Stripes floating over Portsmouth Square and snorted, "That damn rag again!" But the Mormons were a practical and optimistic flock. They had brought with them what "The Old Saw" described as "The most heterogeneous mass of materials ever crowded together... a representative for every mortal thing the mind of man had ever conceived," and they quickly set about improving their lot.

No Mormon was more intent upon self-improvement than Sam Brannan, whose life and times would be a barometer of the changes about to transform Yerba Buena. Brannan was eager to make the best of what seemed a bad lot. In short order, he performed the village's first American marriage (Lizzie Winner betrothed to Basil Hall) and with presses brought from New York, conjured up the town's first newspaper, the *California Star*.

Sam Brannan was soon Yerba Buena's most unhidden and outspoken citizen. Hardly the picture of a church elder, he swaggered down the village's streets in elegant suits and a beaver hat. His relations with the other Mormons had never been entirely pacific, and to his list of firsts was

Builders and boosters: This 1850s group photo captures a self-satisfied bunch of the city's panjandrums. Sam Brannan (upper right) may be the most satisfied of them all.

added the distinction of becoming Yerba Buena's first defendant in a court of law under American jurisdiction. The complaint was misuse of church funds. Later, confronted by the charge that the money he had been extracting was not going to the Lord, he replied loftily, "Go tell Brigham Young that I'll give up the money when he sends me a receipt signed by the Lord." Brannan was acquitted, but he was never far from the scene of an argument.

Sam Brannan's next wrangle had to do with the village's name. Yerba Buena was fine with Brannan and his *Star*, but the town's appointed *alcalde* (mayor), Lt. Washington A. Bartlett, had decreed on January 30, 1847 that Yerba Buena should henceforth be known as San Francisco—thereby, he hoped, linking it with the much better known San Francisco Bay. Bartlett's decision forestalled a similar move by a prominent early settler, Thomas O. Larkin, and Bear Flagger Robert Semple, who had planned to build a town on land at the Carquinez Strait sold to them by General Vallejo. They had wanted to call their city Francisca, after the General's wife. When Bartlett headed them off, they renamed it Benicia, her second name. Tiny Benicia, a hardy little metropolis manqué, still exists, and has a population of about 9,000.

History has had a way of passing Benicia by: in 1853 it served briefly as California's capital, but a year later the capital was transferred to Sacramento.

Bartlett's foresight was lost on Sam Brannan, who ranted and editorialized against the name change. His opposition was ignited by a fierce dislike for "our self-styled, unlimited prerogative *alcalde*." In the end, Bartlett had his way, though Brannan waited three months before he datelined the *Star* San Francisco.

In July Bartlett was formally elected *alcalde* in San Francisco's first election, the first of many to be marred by charges of ballot-box stuffing. He enlisted Jasper O'Farrell, an Irish civil engineer, to expand an 1839 survey of the town. O'Farrell followed the neat but unimaginative grid patterns of the earlier survey, and expanded San Francisco's theoretical area to about 800 acres. But O'Farrell's most noticeable legacy was the creation of Market Street, a hundred-foot wide thoroughfare that linked Yerba Buena Cove with Mission Dolores to the southwest. Market Street cut an angled swath through the grids. In the early days, its irregularity had little effect, but when the city grew it became a booby trap for city planners, teamsters, and, later, for motorists.

In 1847 San Francisco's population was 459, not including military and naval personnel. A hundred ships a year were entering the Golden Gate. Boosters like Brannan were sure that fortune was readying a smile: on March 13 the *Star* commented that the settlement was "now rapidly improving and bids fair to rival in rapidity of progress the most thriving town or city on the American continent."

A Short History of San Francisco

The *Star* was right. San Francisco was still isolated and humble, a mere 150 or so buildings and tents strewn around a muddy cove at the tip of a windy, sandy, and disconcertingly hilly peninsula. But, at the beginning of the fateful year 1848, a man named James W. Marshall, working on a saw-mill in the Sierra foothills, picked up a few flakes of gold and the future of San Francisco was fixed. Marshall's discovery began one of the most enchanting and riproaring events in human history, the California Gold Rush.

The Gold Rush

2

For more than two centuries, the Western World had been awaiting the discovery of a true El Dorado, a country of gold for the taking. When news of Marshall's discovery spread, it was as if a giant bell had rung, signaling the beginning of a furious race to fortune. The myth of El Dorado sprang suddenly to life.

Thousands of men (and a very few women) dropped what they were doing, collected whatever they thought might be of some use in mysterious California, and jumped on any boat or wagon that promised to get them there. Off to "see the elephant," off to California where the gold was plated with gold.

But James Marshall—back on January 24, 1848—had no idea of the avalanche of Argonauts about to descend on the languid hills and valleys of inland California. Marshall had been hired by John Augustus Sutter to build a sawmill on Sutter's property at present-day Coloma, about 115 miles northeast of San Francisco. Sutter, formerly a Swiss Army officer, had arrived in California in 1839 and become a Mexican citizen. Two years later, he was given a 50,000 acre land grant in the Central Valley.

"In character," California's iconoclastic historian Josiah Royce wrote in 1886, "Sutter was an affable and hospitable visionary, of hazy ideas, with a great liking for popularity, and with a mania for undertaking too much." What he had undertaken was nothing less than the creation of a giant personal bailiwick which he called New Helvetia. As the capital of his domain, Sutter built a fort on the site of what is now Sacramento. From there he ruled over his 50,000 acres as a benevolent despot, using Indians as serfs, providing employment for settlers like John Bidwell, and greeting trans-Sierran travelers, for whom Sutter's Fort was often the first breath of civilization in California.

Since the early 1600s, the Spanish had been searching for El Dorado (the Gilded One), an Indian chief in Columbia who supposedly coated himself with gold dust. In time El Dorado came to mean an entire region of gold, for which the Spaniards—and a lot of other people—never stopped looking.

Opposite page
The Argonaut hordes: Hours of digging, panning, rocking, and sluicing might make one an instant millionaire. Or perhaps not.

One of Sutter's hazier ideas was the building of a wood mill on the South Fork of the American River, upstream from his fort. Bidwell wrote that "rafting sawed lumber down the cañons of the American River [was such a] wild ... scheme ... that no other man than Sutter would have been confiding and credulous to believe it practical." But the strong currents of the American and the countless other streams that drain the Sierra are well-suited to other uses than floating wood. As they cut through the rock of the foothills, those streams erode the veins of gold that streak through almost every part of the state.

So it happened that James Marshall (who, Bidwell said, "could turn his hand to almost anything," despite being "half crazy or harebrained") looked into the newly built millrace that day in January and picked up a piece of shiny material, one of the billions of bits of gold that had been gaily tumbling down the river for centuries. Marshall took his nugget—the Wimmer nugget—to Sutter, the two "applied every test of their ingenuity and the American Encyclopedia," and decided that, yes, indeed, they had found gold. And when they went back to the mill and poked and panned awhile, they saw that there was more, much more, to be had.

The Wimmer nugget was named for Marshall's assistant, Peter L. Wimmer. It can be seen today at the Bancroft Library of the University of California, Berkeley. The American River has changed course many times since the 1840s, but a reconstructed sawmill and a pleasant Gold Rush museum are to be found in Coloma today.

John Sutter was a man with a disorderly past, both in his native Europe and in the New World. But he had finally reached a measure of prosperity and respectability as chieftain of New Helvetia. He sensed that his barony would be swamped by gold seekers if word of the discovery escaped, and he swore his workers to silence. But the incendiary news began to filter out when those workers started using gold as payment at Sutter's Fort, California's major inland way station and probably the worst place in the state to keep a secret.

On March 15 the *Californian* (the state's first newspaper, recently moved to San Francisco from Monterey) announced the seismic discovery in a brief paragraph on its back page. The *Californian* took a conservative view (after all, there had been many false alarms, all over the world and right here in California): "Great chances [exist] for scientific capitalists," the paper commented.

On March 24, young E. C. Kemble, Sam Brannan's editor at the *Star*, took a pleasant seven-day river voyage up to the mill to check out the crackling rumors. Sutter took Kemble on a careful tour. The workers, who had been using every free moment to pan gold, were shown industriously building the mill. Kemble returned to San Francisco and wrote that the discovery was a "sham ... a takein ... got up to guzzle the gullible."

But the rumors wouldn't die, and bits of gold kept popping up: at the fort, along the riverway, and in San Francisco. As John Bidwell laconically

A Short History of San Francisco

wrote, "As a lumber enterprise the [mill] was a failure but as a gold discovery it was a grand success." Finally, on May 12, Sam Brannan put on his beaver hat and paraded himself and a vial of gold dust down Montgomery Street, crying "Gold! Gold! Gold on the American River!"

Rumor had it that Brannan's store at Sutter's Fort was well and newly stocked with mining gear in advance of his historic march. But the Gold Rush stunned almost everybody else. In a flash the little town of San Francisco was almost deserted. The *Californian* ceased publishing—its staff was on its way to the hills. Goods were left piled up at Yerba Buena Cove, as there was no one left to pack them. Even the grog shops were emptied, as nearly every ambulatory human being in San Francisco rushed off to the gold country. The news spread up and down California; within a few days Monterey and the other mission towns had joined the scramble. The fever spread to Utah, and into Oregon, where, one observer wrote, "two-thirds of [the state's] able-bodied men were on their way to the diggings."

The few merchants who remained in San Francisco quickly sold out of picks, shovels, food, clothes, canvas, lanterns, anything and everything the gold seekers thought they might need. Frantic orders to Hawaii for supplies spread the word around the Pacific Basin. Peru and Chile, Hawaii, and Australia began to send prospectors.

News travelled east, notably in the form of a "small chest called a caddy containing $3,000 worth of gold in lumps and scales," carried by one Lt. L. Loeser. In November the caddy was temptingly displayed at the War Office in Washington, D.C. And, on December 2, President Polk, in his last message to Congress, gave the Gold Rush an official endorsement: "The accounts of gold in [California] are of such an extraordinary character as would scarcely command belief were it not corroborated by the authentic reports of officers in the public service who visited the mineral district, and derived the facts which they detail from personal observation." Four days later, the New York *Herald* summed up the excitement, "The El Dorado of the old Spaniards is discovered at last."

"Gold Fever," historian John Walton Caughey has written, "swept the Atlantic seaboard, jarred staid New England, coursed through the Ohio Valley, and up and down the Mississippi . . . spread to Canada, jumped the Atlantic to England, invaded the European continent and stirred France and Germany, the Baltic peoples, and the Mediterranean." Along the way gold fever infected hundreds of thousands of farmers, students, loafers, shopkeepers, scoundrels, clerks, and solid citizens. But the spout of the funnel of this auriferous longing, the gateway to the diggings, namely the muddy village of San Francisco was, in 1849, on the other side of the world—

whatever side of the world one started from.

Prentice Mulford, later an outstanding San Francisco literary figure, was living in the little Long Island town of Sag Harbor when the news came roaring in. During the long winter of 1848–49 there was talk of little else. California, Mulford later wrote in his classic *Prentice Mulford's Story*, "was but a blotch of yellow on the schoolboy's map . . . the Sacramento River was reported as abounding in alligators . . . the general opinion was that it was a fearfully hot country and full of snakes."

Ways to El Dorado: The newly minted argonauts soon found that there were three routes to San Francisco (once they found their way to America). The first Forty-Niners came via the Isthmus of Panama. Ships up and down the eastern seaboard were loaded with buzzing would-be miners and sailed to the Atlantic port of Chagres, described by one writer as "a fifty hut cesspool of matted reeds thatched with palm leaves." From Chagres the prospectors made their way by horseback and canoe through the dripping, mosquito- and disease-ridden jungle. At the end of the dismal trek was the tatty little Pacific town of Panama, "another lecherous tropical excrescence . . . brought out of listless living once more by golden treasure." There they piled up nervously and awaited a ship, any ship, to take them up the coast to San Francisco.

The trail from Chagres to Panama was an ancient one: it had been used centuries earlier by the Spanish returning home in the opposite direction with Peruvian gold.

The Panama route was the quickest way to the gold fields, especially after a railway was built, cutting travel time from four days to a few hours. From New York to San Francisco via Panama usually took six to eight weeks, but it was expensive and in time became the rich man's route.

Passage by ship from the east, around Cape Horn at the southern tip of South America, then up the Pacific coast to San Francisco, was longer but cheaper. During the four- to eight-month voyage, passengers put up with wormy rations, unpredictable seas, and dictatorial captains. To while away the time, they formed theatrical societies and debating clubs, published on-board newspapers, and meditated on the best ways to spend all the money waiting for them in Golden California.

It was a dangerous voyage (between 1851 and 1853, eleven ships were lost at Cape Horn), and getting past the icy, horrifyingly stormy Cape could be agonizing—the *Golden Eagle* spent three months butting up against adverse winds. More than one captain gave up and sailed to California the long way, via the Orient. Nevertheless, from mid-December 1848 (shortly after President Polk's stunning announcement) to mid-January 1849, more than sixty ships left eastern ports for California. More and more Forty-

Niners were clamoring to ship out, sometimes paying for the privilege of working as crew, buying boats, renting them, or hauling them out of retirement. From January to February, 120 more ships left for the diggings. By Fall, 600 ships lay in San Francisco harbor. Two years later, 774 were counted, "most of them deserted"—gold fever having infected passengers, crew, and captains alike.

In the first three years of the Gold Rush, more than 200,000 men (and women and even a few children) came to California—one of the greatest peaceful mass migrations in history. Half came by sea, by the Isthmus or the Cape. The other half chose the long, dry overland route.

There was simply no easy way to get to California, but many Forty-Niners already owned wagons, equipment, and stock and lived relatively close to the jumping-off points of St. Joseph and Independence, Missouri, or Council Bluffs, Iowa. There were a number of possible overland routes, but most wagon trains (in numbers there being a measure of safety) set off in April or May, and followed the shallow ribbon of the Platte River across Nebraska, counting off the awaited landmarks: Court House Rocks, Chimney Rock, Scotts Bluff, Independence Rock. The trains skirted north of the Rockies in Wyoming through South Pass, just south of the forbidding Wind River Range and then dropped down to the Great Salt Lake, where they could resupply and perhaps trade stories about the Mormons, whose extraordinary beliefs and polygamous practices were considered little short of exotic. After Salt Lake, the worst part of the journey began, the crossing of the Great Basin.

A broken axle, a sick animal, an attack of cholera or Indians could mean death for the overlanders. But what one Forty-Niner named Alonzo Delano called "the magic talisman of gold" was terribly powerful, and the waterless trail was crowded with impatient sufferers from gold fever. Delano described the scene from a crest near the Platte:

> For miles, to the extent of vision, an animated mass of beings broke upon our view. Long trains of wagons with their white covers were moving slowly along, a multitude of horsemen were prancing on the road, companies of men were travelling on foot, and although the scene was not a gorgeous one, yet the display of banners from many wagons, and the multitude of armed men, looked as if a mighty army was on its march.

The overlanders hoped to make their crossing of the Sierra Nevada just before the winter snows; the awful example of the anthropophagous Donner Party was never forgotten. The last part of the journey before the

SIOUX INDIANS.

CHASING BUFFALOES, SCOTT'S BLUFFS.

COURT HOUSE ROCK.

CHIMNEY ROCK.

FIRST NIGHT ON THE PLAINS.

LARAMIE PEAK.

SCENE ON THE DESERT.

crossing was the most difficult of all. The land to the east of the Sierra is bare and forbidding. The mountains rise up with frightening steepness. By that time the Forty-Niners, human, beast, and wagon, were bitterly tired. But at the high crest of the Sierra, after a deadly uphill slog, the Argonauts looked down the green and gentle western slope. Hoots and hollers, tears and prayers; after months of harsh desert, a deliverance. Gold or no gold, California seemed a promised land.

For many of the Forty-Niners, the first sign of civilization was often Sutter's Fort. In earlier days, Sutter had gloried in providing baronial hospitality and succor to overlanders. But after Marshall's discovery, he was forced to watch as New Helvetia and his prosperity were trampled underfoot by them.

Both Marshall and Sutter were ruined by the Gold Rush. Marshall became a kind of human talisman, hounded at every turn by miners convinced that he had a mysterious ability to ferret out rich deposits. He quickly became soured by his inability to cash in on his discovery. In the end, all he had was fame, which he said was "neither victuals nor clothes to anyone." He died broke and broken down near Coloma in 1885.

Sutter's well-documented and, under the terms of the U.S. annexation, entirely legal ownership of New Helvetia, was ignored by squatters to whom a Mexican land grant was just so much quaint nonsense. As Josiah Royce ironically noted, "Providence, you see, and manifest destiny were understood in those days to be on our side, and absolutely opposed to the base Mexican." Sutter's fortunes rose and fell for a few years, but he was finally reduced to insistently petitioning the federal government for reimbursement. He died, despairing, near Philadelphia in 1880.

The Instant City: Whether they came by land or sea, the Forty-Niners were impatient to get up to the diggings, but most first had to visit the suddenly famous, exciting and exotic city of San Francisco. It was instantly and forever the nexus of all the threads of greed and longing and energy that were the Gold Rush. Another town—Benicia, say—might have been the capital of it all. As it was, goods and people had to be transhipped from San Francisco across to the East Bay, or down the Peninsula and then east to the "Mother Lode." And some ships sailed directly through the Carquinez towards the new town of Sacramento, abuilding at the site of Sutter's Fort. But from the day Sam Brannan issued his booming invitation to the world, San Francisco was the City of Gold.

Not all of the 50,000 or so people who arrived in San Francisco in 1849

Opposite page
The lure of gold: The overland route was long, dry and dangerous—but often the cheapest way to the goldfields.

The would-be baron: John Sutter's central California realm was quickly overrun by goldseekers.

were lured simply by gold. Some came to help satisfy the various lusts of what Mark Twain called "a wild, free, disorderly, grotesque society! Men— only swarming hosts of stalwart *men*—nothing juvenile, nothing feminine visible anywhere." Some began laying the orderly framework for the city San Francisco seemed sure to become. And some came to marvel and to report.

One such was a young and hardy reporter for the *New York Tribune* named Bayard Taylor. Taylor had already made a reputation for himself with a book about his rambles "With Knapsack and Staff" in Europe. When gold fever in New York got "worse than the cholera," he convinced the *Tribune's* legendary editor Horace Greeley to send him to California.

Taylor landed in San Francisco in September 1849, after a fifty-one-day voyage from New York via the Isthmus. In his classic book *El Dorado*, Taylor gave one of the best descriptions of the fantastic village-cum-metropolis. He first noted:

> Hundreds of tents and houses . . . scattered all over the heights, and along the shore for over a mile. A furious wind was blowing through a gap in the hills, filling the streets with clouds of dust. On every side stood buildings of all kinds, begun or half-finished, and the greater part of them mere canvas sheds, open in front and covered with all kinds of signs in all languages. Great quantities of goods were piled up in the open air, for want of a place to store them. The streets were full of people, hurrying to and fro, and of divers and bizarre a character as the houses: Yankees of every possible variety, native Californians in sarapes and sombreros, Chilians, Sonorians, Kanakas from Hawaii, Chinese with long tails, Malays armed with their everlasting creeses, and others in whose embronzed and bearded visages it was impossible to recognize any especial nationality.

After paying porters two dollars apiece to deposit his luggage at a cramped and dingy rooming house ("a sum so immense . . . that there was no longer any doubt of our having landed in California"), the 26-year-old reporter settled in for a short stay before heading up to the diggings.

The San Francisco Taylor saw was the prototypical boom town. Gold dust scented the air. New and old money, ambition, and a bone-deep sense of adventure fueled a nonstop machine of excitement and anticipation. Gambling, in tents, shanties, and in the few wooden structures on the sandy hills, was a mania. John Henry Brown, a raconteur and innkeeper of Yerba Buena vintage, recalled years later, "I have known many a gambler to pay for a loan of money as high as ten per cent per hour."

Speculation of all kinds was epidemic. One of Taylor's shipmates sold

1,500 copies of the *Tribune* "in two hours at one dollar apiece." Real estate (then, now, and probably forevermore) was a prime source of speculative frenzy. Taylor wrote that "a friend of mine, who wished to find a place for a law practice, was shown a cellar in the earth about twelve feet square and six deep, which he could have for $250 a month."

"A perpetual carnival reigns," wrote another visitor (though he was "sure no other city contains so many rogues and cut-throats"). The San Francisco eccentric, driven slightly off-track by the sheer wonder of it all, was already in evidence. "One man who went by the name Dancing Billy," John Henry Brown recalled, "would station himself on the front verandah, and dance by the hour and would only stop long enough to treat all who would spend their time looking at him. I know of the instance where he gave a man 50 dollars to play for him one hour."

Taylor himself was a little stunned by San Francisco's outlandishness. But not everyone found the city to their taste. One visitor called it "a vast garbage heap... this is the most abhorrent place a man could live." The Frenchman Albert Bernard de Russailh complained that a night with one of San Francisco's "women of easy virtue costs from $200 to $400... there are some honest women in San Francisco," he wrote, "but not very many."

But even with the cutthroats and inflated prices, it was a unique and heady place. Taylor, caught up in the excitement, wrote, "One knows not whether he is awake or in some wonderful dream. Never before have I had the difficulty in establishing satisfactorily to my own sense, the reality of what I saw and heard."

To the Diggings: After a few days in San Francisco, Bayard Taylor set out on horseback for the gold fields, dressed in "Chilean spurs with rowels two inches long... and [a] Mexican serape." The intoxicating carnival of San Francisco was, after all, an effect, and a good reporter like Taylor had to visit the cause, the land of gold itself. His route was typical: down the San Francisco Peninsula, then east across the Central Valley (passing through the fledgling San Joaquin River port of Stockton) and up into the oak-covered foothills of the Sierra Nevada, where the Argonaut hordes sought their fortune.

In the summer it was a hot journey but not an especially trying one. As a Forty-Niner named E. G. Waite put it, "The very color of the earth, covered with wild oats or dried grass, suggested a land of gold."

Gold has been found at one time or another almost everywhere in California. But most of the 120,000 or so aurophiles concentrated on the

Gold has been found in fifty-two of California's fifty-eight counties. San Francisco County (the only joint city/county in the state) figures among those not so blessed.

The Gold Rush

A. Mother Lode
B. Donner Pass
C. Coloma
D. Sutter's Fort
E. Mariposa

It is impossible to translate the dollar values of the gold mined in the 1840s and 50s into contemporary terms with any accuracy. Perhaps more important than the figures is the fact that the Mother Lode's gold was responsible for setting San Francisco and California on their way as financial giants.

fabled Mother Lode, stretching from north of Sutter's Mill to Mariposa in the south, a distance of about 120 miles. Because the Mother Lode was relatively narrow (from two miles to a few hundred yards wide), it was thought that there was indeed a single vein of gold running parallel to the Sierra. In fact, the fissures of gold were scattered about unpredictably. But few miners cared much for the finer points of geology: gold, for the first few years anyway, seemed easy enough to find.

The once quiet hills were boiling with starry-eyed Forty-Niners. When Bayard Taylor "first saw men, carrying heavy stones in the sun, standing nearly waist-deep in water and grubbing with their hands in the gravel and clay," he thought he might be immune to gold fever. "But when the shining particles were poured out lavishly from a tin basin, I confess there was a sudden itching in my fingers to seize the nearest crowbar and biggest shovel."

It sometimes seemed that you could make your first fortune just "poking around with a knife." In the giddy first years of the Gold Rush, though, the most popular method of finding the precious stuff was panning. In time miners began using sluices—in effect, pans made large. And later, when most of the virgin or placer gold had been plucked out of the streams and sandbars of the diggings, capital-intensive hydraulic mining was required. It was such high-technology mining, in fact, that in the long term accounted for most of the wealth that flowed out of the Mother Lode. And wealth there was: $10 million was taken out of the hills in 1849, $40 million in 1850, up to a peak of over $80 million in 1852.

It may have been capitalists in San Francisco and the east who in the end pocketed most of the Mother Lode's wealth. But the popular image of the Gold Rush has always been that of the optimistic, fiercely independent miner, squatting by a stream in his floppy hat and patchy clothes, panning gold. That was what Bayard Taylor saw when he visited the diggings in late 1849 when optimism and energy were high.

For the shopkeepers, clerks, farmers, and assorted birds of passage who comprised the Forty-Niners, panning had the virtue of utter simplicity. The miner scooped up a quantity of stream gravel in his pan and, turning and shifting and muttering, let the heavy gold sink to the bottom while the debris washed away. A hardworking Forty-Niner might account for fifty pans a day. His take in nuggets and dust and scales depended on luck.

The Forty-Niners roamed the Mother Lode, looking for the claim, perhaps *the* great claim, that would make them rich. Like panning, staking a claim was a simple matter. The land was owned by the federal government, but in practice the miners were allowed to claim a reasonable amount of land (depending on the terrain), provided they actually worked their claim. This ruled out speculation and helped give the early diggings their colorfully individualistic flavor. Few men cared to make another man rich when riches were all around.

Bayard Taylor was impressed by the orderliness of it all. "The capacity of people for self-government was never so triumphantly illustrated," he wrote. "Nothing in California seemed more miraculous than this spontaneous evolution of social order from the worst elements of anarchy." Indeed California claim law, built up of little theory and much practice, was transplanted to every gold strike in the American West.

The occasional dispute over a claim was usually settled by an elected claims officer, called a recorder or *alcalde*. And if a miner's claim was disallowed, it was a simple matter for one of those energetic young men (over half the Forty-Niners were in their twenties) to gather up his kit and cross over the ridge to the next canyon.

By 1851 over 500 Gold Rush towns had blossomed in the canyons and flats and meadows of the diggings. Their names are fragrant with the rough romance of Gold Rush life: Rich Bar, Port Wine, Kanaka Creek, Greenhorn Bar, Humbug Hill, and Hangtown. Some of these little settlements—collections of tents, perhaps a few wood shanties—lasted only a season; some, like Hangtown (Placerville), exist today. They were refuges from the mud and snow of winter, places where the miners could buy supplies, trade gossip and fantasies, and gamble their newfound fortunes in the "hells."

It was an overwhelmingly male population, and what women there were weren't likely to figure prominently in letters home. But, despite their rough appearance, many of the Forty-Niners were civilized fellows, easterners many of them, used to culture and society. So they formed theatrical groups and literary clubs, and some even spent the traditionally work-free Sundays reading the Bible. Dances were held ("the 'women' you could tell by the ribbons on the men's arms") and occasionally a theatrical group would come to call—perhaps the deliciously scandalous Lola Montez or the Junius Brutus Booth family (including young John Wilkes), who offered high-toned Shakespearean productions to the hooting, novelty-starved miners.

The world, for good reason, was amazed and intrigued by the Gold Rush. Bayard Taylor's reports to the *Tribune* were a sensation. The younger Alexander Dumas ventured west and described the new wonderland in a book, *Un an sur les bords du San Joaquin et du Sacramento*. Even Heinrich Schliemann came to California, took American citizenship, and later wrote of his experiences (which included making the fortune that bankrolled his successful expeditions in search of the lost city of Troy).

The Gold Rush

Not every observer was edified by the migration to the American El Dorado. Thomas De Quincey, author of *Confessions of an English Opium-Eater*, compared the Gold Rush to the Children's Crusade, and called it "a swindle . . . a regular conspiracy of jobbers." And Henry David Thoreau was appalled. "It makes God to be a moneyed gentleman," he wrote, "who scatters a handful of pennies in order to see mankind scramble for them. Going to California. It is only three thousand miles closer to hell."

However far from hell it was, the Gold Rush quickly became folklore. And why not? The elements that made up the story were inescapably romantic: courageous, ambitious young men pitted against a remote wilderness, making and losing fortunes, building a wonderful and beautiful city, all against the fascinating backdrop of gold.

In later years, writers like Mark Twain and Bret Harte took the complex reality of the Gold Rush and fashioned a tidy and enduring myth. Harte especially (though he came late to the almost worked-out diggings), created a romantic, comic picture of Gold Rush life. His stories were peopled by golden-hearted prostitutes, cynical gamblers capable of noble self-sacrifice, as in *The Outcasts of Poker Flat*, and rough-hewn miners cooing over orphaned babies, as in his most famous story, *The Luck of Roaring Camp*.

"In all my personal experience in mining camps from 1849 to 1854, there was not a case of bloodshed, robbery, theft or actual violence," wrote E.G. Waite, ordinarily a reliable witness. But Waite also mentioned an occasional need for "courageous and brawny 49ers" to take "pistol in hand to right a grievous wrong to a stranger."

It made for a good story and much of it had a rich vein of truth. But the Gold Rush had another side to it. There was too much money floating around the Mother Lode for theft and mayhem to be absent. "Yesterday one American shot another in the street and the occurrence was not noticed as much as a dog fight back home," wrote one visitor. Louise Clapp, one of the few fine-grained ladies in the hills, described life in the diggings in a series of letters to her sister back east, letters that became famous as "The Shirley Letters" when published in San Francisco. "In one short space of twenty-four hours," she wrote, "we have had murders, fearful accidents, bloody deaths, a mob, whippings, a hanging, an attempt at suicide and a fatal duel." That was surely an extraordinary twenty-four hours (and all those carryings-on were part of a single skein of violence), but the diggings were clearly no place for the faint of heart.

Then, too, in the midst of that "triumphant . . . evolution of social order," there was the problem of racism. The gentlefolk of the ranches were contemptuously swept aside by the first Argonauts. Even Taylor conceded that "the first colony of gold hunters attempted to drive out all foreigners without distinction, as well as native Californians." When the Foreign Miners' Tax was enacted in 1850 it became nearly impossible for non-Americans (and perhaps a few Frenchmen, Germans, or Englishmen) to mine. Blacks and native Indians were excluded as a matter of course, unless they worked as slaves or semislaves.

It was a hard life. Disease had its way and so did despair. One doctor estimated that one in five newcomers died within six months of arrival. As E. G. Waite wrote, mining was "a species of gambling. The short duration of a placer claim, the loss of time in finding another, and the too general restlessness, tell the story of too many failures to realize a fortune by even those who were the most lucky. Too often it was due to extravagance, gambling, or the guzzling of brandy or whiskey at eight dollars a bottle. But, drunk or sober, one was obliged to pay two ounces [about $32] for a pair of pantaloons, a hundred dollars for a pair of long-legged boots, and four dollars expressage for a letter."

Years later, Mark Twain asked of the Forty-Niners, "Where are they now? Scattered to the ends of the earth—or prematurely aged and decrepit—or shot or stabbed in street afrays—or dead of disappointed hopes and broken hearts—all gone, or nearly all—victims devoted upon the altar of the golden calf—the noblest holocaust that ever wafted its sacrificial incense heavenward. It is pitiful to think upon."

But that was Mark Twain in one of his dark moods. Certainly the truth of the Gold Rush lies somewhere between Twain's morbidity and the romanticism of Bret Harte (and Twain himself in brighter times—witness "The Celebrated Jumping Frog of Calaveras County.") The Gold Rush, after all, was a great adventure—for many, the great adventure of a lifetime.

Bayard Taylor is a case in point. After the Gold Rush, he travelled extensively, wrote voluminously in prose and poetry. (His translation of Goethe's *Faust* is still considered a standard.) But he never again achieved the success that *El Dorado* brought him. The Gold Rush was a crucible of experience. As Taylor wrote, "a man could no more expect to retain his old nature unchanged than he could retain in his lungs the air he had breathed on the Atlantic shore."

For many generations, the only equivalent of its raw excitement—the opportunity to test oneself, to flee the ordinary—has been war. The Gold Rush may have been a celebration of base greed, but it was no war.

An exception to the rule imposed by the Foreign Miners' Tax was Chinese Camp, center of an area mined by an estimated 5,000 Chinese in the early 1850s. In 1856 more than 2,000 "Celestials" engaged in a great tong battle near the town. It must have been largely ritualistic in nature, since only four fatalities—perhaps accidental—were reported.

The "Actual Metropolis"

3

Most of the gold flowing down the streams of the foothills and in and out of the pockets of the Forty-Niners tended, by some barely mutable man-made law, to find its way to the budding city by the Bay. San Francisco was the magnet, not only for the wealth of the diggings, but also for the aspirations of what Josiah Royce approvingly called "the conservative social elements."

From the beginning of the Gold Rush, there was no doubt that San Francisco was destined for greatness. Bayard Taylor repeated the common wisdom when he wrote, "There is more gold in California than was ever said or imagined . . . ages will not exhaust the supply." San Francisco was the obvious haven for that gold. "Here," wrote Royce, "the young state was . . . nourished. Here the ships and a great part of the immigrants came. Here from the first was the center of the state's mental life . . . the progress of San Francisco was to be largely identical with the progress of the whole of the new state."

When Taylor first saw San Francisco in September 1849, he was staggered by the frenzy of expansion going on in all quarters. And when he returned four months later from the gold fields, the city hadn't stopped progressing for a precious instant. "Of all the marvelous phases of the present," he wrote, "the growth of San Francisco is the one which will most tax the belief of the future."

Instead of the "scattering town of tents and canvas houses with a show of frame buildings on one or two streets and a population of about six thousand," he found "an actual metropolis, displaying street after street of well built edifices." On his first visit, the city still huddled around Yerba Buena Cove and the bottoms of the hills. Now, it "stretched to the topmost heights [and] followed the shore around point after point." The first arrivals

California was admitted to the Union with ferocious haste on September 9, 1850. As Josiah Royce pointed out, San Francisco was the focal point of the state—practically synonymous with it—until well into this century, when Los Angeles, San Diego and other burgs began edging out from its shadow.

Opposite page
Tents and shanties: San Francisco in 1849, in the first months of its fantastic boom, already bore little resemblance to muddy Yerba Buena village (see page 19).

"lodged in muslin rooms and canvas garrets with a philosophic lack of furniture, and ate [their] simple though substantial fare from pine boards. Now lofty hotels, gaudy with verandahs and balconies were met with [everywhere], furnished with home luxury, and aristocratic restaurants presented daily their long bills of fare, rich with the choicest technicalities of Parisian cuisine."

No one had the leisure to conduct a census, but Taylor estimated that the town's population had grown from 6,000 to 30,000 in four months. Most San Franciscans were peppy young men; though there were a few thousand "feminines" in the city at the time, it wasn't until the 1880s that women comprised even a third of San Francisco's population. "The great want of San Francisco was society," Taylor wrote delicately.

The "plentiful lack of women and children" had an unsettling effect on some. One writer related that "Judge S. told us that when he arrived in 1849, and walked up from the ship with his wife and several little children, men crowded about the children, asking permission to kiss them, to shake hands with them, to give them gold specimens out of their chamois skin sacks, or a little gold dust to make them rings or something for an ornament, following them a long way."

There was little soft and pretty in early San Francisco. Every need was immediate. Land and wharves were in short supply, so shallow Yerba Buena Cove was filled in with what one writer called "conglomerate layers of cook stoves, boxes of tobacco, Chilean flour, barrels of spoiled beef, rolls of sheet lead, gold-washing machines, tons of wine sieves, discarded clothing [and] a slight covering of earth." Many of the hundreds of ships that lay deserted in the harbor were sunk to create landfill.

Ships spared the indignity of being used as landfill were converted into hotels, stores, and, in the case of the *Euphemia*, a much-needed jail and refuge for lunatics. In the first frantic days, landfill was just tossed out onto the tidal mudflat. After 1851 much of the reclaiming was done by "steam paddies," earth-moving machines so called because one could replace a whole crew of Irishmen. Soon forty square blocks—much of today's financial district—had been reclaimed.

Only one thing mattered in those early days: money. How to grab on to some of the torrent of gold that was streaming out of the diggings into the new city. There evolved a democracy of happy greed, a down-to-earthness in which "the philosopher abandoned the limitless void to become a toiler in the solid mass of reality." The man who carried your bags might be a bored Pennsylvania judge; the saloon fiddler, the scion of some worried eastern family. Bayard Taylor saw the spirit in one eatery, "There are cries of

Some might wonder whether the rampant maleness of early San Francisco was an augury of the city's latter-day "gay" subculture. The early chroniclers, whether from obtuseness or prudery, give no hints. One might imagine that such homo-sexuals as were to be found in San Francisco thought it, as always, a more tolerant place than most.

Sunken ships will occasionally be unearthed during excavation for a new building in downtown San Francisco. One such was the *Niantic*, variously a Panama emigrant ship, a warehouse, and a hotel. In May 1978 the remains of the *Niantic* were found during construction of an office building at Clay and Sansome. For three days work was held up while archaeologists dug up a wealth of Gold Rush artifacts. An eight-foot cross-section of the *Niantic's* rotten hull was removed before the old ship was finally plowed under forever.

A Short History of San Francisco

'Steward!' from all parts . . . the word waiter is not considered sufficiently respectable seeing that the waiter may have been a lawyer or merchant's clerk a few months before.''

Except for a few well-stuffed dandies like Sam Brannan, most of those young gents looked much the same. They were a chronically scruffy lot, their boots caked with mud, their thick woolen shirts redolent of work and play. They wore their slouched hats over tangled hair and might have sported a pair of blue denim pants with copper rivets, newly invented in 1850 by a 20-year-old German-born immigrant named Levi Strauss. The town they graced was rough, masculine, and breathless with the promise of money and adventure.

Money Madness: All that gold sharpened Yankee wits. The town was a cauldron of buying, selling, and speculation on what hadn't quite arrived yet. Distances were so great and the city's needs so unpredictable that Eastern merchants were simply filling up boats with whatever they thought might sell in San Francisco and sending them off with a prayer. Months later, those ships would land in the cove, tie up at one of the rickety new piers and put up their cargo for auction.

If the goods were in short supply, the merchants stood to get rich. If not, and there was a temporary surplus of tea or rice or nails or flour or pianos, the crates so laboriously brought around Cape Horn might end up being tossed into the Bay as mere landfill or onto the streets to provide walkways in the wintry mud. California's great pioneer historian Hubert Howe Bancroft told the story of how ''when tobacco was down, a man desirous of building a house on made ground [landfill] tumbled in boxes of it, enough to form a foundation. Before the house was built tobacco was worth $1 a pound, more than a dozen such houses.''

The truly crafty and cool-hearted went in for the great game of cornering the market. As Bancroft put it, ''the trick was to get goods, not to sell them.'' A fortune could be made by keeping a wakeful eye on the Golden Gate, racing out in a dinghy to a newly arrived ship and frantically buying up a whole cargo before the bemused captain quite knew what was happening. Sam Brannan once cornered the tea market, and Taylor told the story of a man who ''purchased all the candlewick to be found, at an average price of 40 cts. per lb. and sold it in a short time for $2.25 per lb.''

Each Pacific wind seemed to blow inspiration into the ear of some ambitious gent. Old John Henry Brown recalled the man who did the sweeping at the City Hotel barroom. He ''would save the sweepings in a

In mid-1850 a semaphore station was established on Telegraph Hill (hence its name) to signal the arrival and type of ships entering the Golden Gate. The story has it that on one occasion an actor who spread his arms wide on stage and exclaimed, ''What means this, my Lord?'' was greeted with the response ''Sidewheel steamer!'' from the audience.

barrel, until full; and on washing it out he obtained over two hundred dollars in gold dust." Two Tammany Hall politicos from New York named Fred Kohler and David Broderick hit upon an even more interesting way to make money. Kohler and Broderick saw that there was a great need for acceptable, standardized currency. So they manufactured gold slugs and cleared gratifying profits by using $4 of gold in their $5 slugs and $8 in their $10 denominations.

Broderick was a good specimen of the turbulence of Gold Rush life. Well-equipped mentally and monetarily, he went into politics when the federal government relieved the coin shortage by opening a mint on Commercial Street in 1854. In 1857 he was elected to the United States Senate, his trail to that august chamber having been liberally sprinkled with gold dust. Two years later, he was killed in an unequal duel by a fiery Texan named David S. Terry. Until the day before the duel, Terry had been chief justice of the California Supreme Court.

For every high-roller like Brannan and Broderick, there were a hundred slightly less dramatic schemers. There were those making a bundle ferrying water across the Bay from the village of Sausalito and selling it in often parched San Francisco for ten cents a pail. Or those who sailed out to the rookeries of the Farallon Islands, gathered eggs, and sold them for a dollar apiece. Common laborers were making a lavish "ounce" ($16 or so) a day, and a good way for the city's few women to make money (outside of less cleansing pursuits) was to set up a laundry. The need was so great that some Forty-Niners sent their laundry to Hawaii and China, or so legend has it. What's sure is that transpacific ships would have been carrying San Francisco's dirty duds to the ends of the planet had there been an ounce of profit in it.

As usual, the wiliest of the new city's entrepreneurs dealt in land. The *Annals of San Francisco*, a lively contemporary chronicle, related that "the richest men in San Francisco have made the best portion of their wealth by the possession of real estate." Land speculators had a friend in San Francisco's impoverished, overwhelmed city government. Aside from the sale of gambling licenses, about the only quick way for the city to raise money was to sell its own land, which speculators, following O'Farrell's survey, subdivided into unimaginative and cramped grid lots. So, instead of streets that follow the graceful contours of the city's hills, San Francisco is stuck with streets that barge up, down and across those hills, as if the whole city were as flat as old Yerba Buena Cove.

Whether it was land, rice, candlewick, or gold, the city was in a constant fever of commerce. Bayard Taylor described the city at midmorning:

The crowd in the streets is now wholly alive. Men dart hither and thither, as if possessed by a never resting spirit. You speak to an acquaintance—a merchant perhaps. He utters a few hurried words of greeting, while his eyes send keen glances on all sides of you, suddenly he catches sight of somebody in the crowd, he is off, and the next five minutes he has bought up half a cargo, sold a town lot at treble the sum he gave, and taken a share in some new and imposing speculation.

In 1851, only two years after the Gold Rush began, San Francisco ranked fourth in the nation in foreign trade (after Boston, New York, and New Orleans) and the city was mustering its first troop of millionaires.

Lick, Brannan, and the Emperor: There were men like the close-mouthed oddball James Lick, who had arrived in Yerba Buena in 1847, aged fifty-one, with $40,000 he had earned selling pianos and hides in the Argentine. No sooner had he arrived in Yerba Buena than Lick began using his hoard to buy up sandy city lots in the village. When the Gold Rush exploded, Lick was instantly and securely a millionaire. But unlike most of the city's rich, Lick was a pinchfist, even to the point of wearing cast-off clothes.

He used his money wisely, though: buying more property, building the city's first luxury hotel, the Lick House, and starting the first fruit orchards in the state. But before he died in 1876, Lick, a bachelor, began giving his money away in a fit of remorse. The miser became a benefactor, giving his millions to the California Society of Pioneers, a trade school, a myriad charities, and the observatory on Mt. Hamilton, south of the city, which possessed the largest telescope in the world (Lick had to be dissuaded from having the telescope built in downtown San Francisco).

While James Lick was skulking about town in eccentric anonymity, Sam Brannan was polishing his reputation as San Francisco's best-known man. He had, after all, been the bringer of the golden tidings, and now, in the words of Samuel Dickson, a great San Francisco story teller, Brannan "shouted and beat on tin pans and made money." He was the city's "herald, its prophet, its spieler, its pitchman."

Brannan's beaver hats and fancy clothes, his lavish parties and hearty charities were funded by a variety of concerns: he owned choice parcels of land, he ran the town's leading newspaper, he gambled assiduously, he owned a flour-mill and cunningly speculated on the avalanche of goods descending on San Francisco. He was the strutting repository of inside

Norton, the First and Only: Emperor Joshua Norton, failed rice speculator, was a boon to bored newsmen for 25 years.

information: whatever he touched seemed to bloom. Dickson wrote that a pie vendor used to hawk his wares with the cry, "Mince pies, apple pies, cheese pies! Everybody buys 'em! Sam Brannan buys 'em."

There were scores of men only slightly less fortunate than Lick and Brannan. As John Henry Brown recalled, "I am almost afraid that you will hardly believe that in those days money could be made so easily in so short a time." And, he might have added, so easily lost.

One big loser in the rough capitalism of the day was a trader by the name of Joshua Abraham Norton, who arrived in San Francisco from South Africa in 1849. He entered the commodities market and by 1853 had amassed a $250,000 fortune. That same year, while the Gold Rush was still boiling and fortune still danced till dawn, Norton tried and failed to corner the rice market. Suddenly dollarless, his senses in disarray, he left town. A few months later, he reappeared in the offices of the *San Francisco Bulletin* and plunked down on the editor's desk a proclamation declaring himself "Emperor of the United States and Protector of Mexico." The *Bulletin* printed Norton's missive and so began the quarter-century rule of the mad Emperor of San Francisco, the darling of the city's newspapers, the living souvenir of Gold Rush folly.

San Francisco has always enjoyed playing the part of tolerant host to eccentrics. In the Emperor Norton, the city found a perfect guest. Norton's proclamations were printed with mock solemnity. His handsomely printed promissory notes (50¢ at five percent interest, due in 1880) were honored everywhere. Tailors vied for the honor and publicity of outfitting the Emperor in his epauletted uniform.

Accompanied everywhere by his faithful mutts Lazarus and Bummer—celebrities in their own right—Emperor Norton strode majestically down San Francisco's streets, accepting the obeisances of his subjects, dropping in on a favored saloon for a free lunch, visiting the board rooms of the city's businesses.

Norton knew, as a successful crackbrain must, how far he could go before tolerance turned to the ungentle solicitude of the loony bin. His proclamations were often witty and carried a little moral, and he rarely overstayed his welcome or forgot the dignity expected of the exalted. In short, he gave good value for the newspaper space, the free lunches, the self-conscious generosity of his subjects.

When Emperor Norton died in 1880—just as his countless promissory notes were coming due—he was given a teary municipal funeral (paid for by the swells of the Pacific Club, later the Pacific Union, then and now the city's most exclusive men's club). Ten thousand people passed by his coffin and a boy's choir sang "Nearer My God To Thee." Not only had a well-loved old man died, so too had a memory of San Francisco's dizzy past.

The Best Bad Things: If everyone in Gold Rush San Francisco who lost their fortune had turned into an Emperor Norton, the city would have quickly been full up and fed up with sovereigns. In those supercharged days, Bayard Taylor wrote, "If a person lost his all, he was perfectly indifferent; two weeks of hard work gave him enough to start on, and two months, with the usual luck, quite reinstated him."

Once reinstated, the new San Franciscan could once again sample the vices and amusements that from the first were part of the city's legend. "I have seen," Hinton Helper wrote in *Land of Gold* in 1855, "purer liquors, better seegars, finer tobacco, truer guns and pistols, larger dirks and bowie knives, and prettier cortezans, here in San Francisco than in any place I have ever visited; and it is my unbiased opinion that California can and does furnish the best bad things that are obtainable in America."

In 1853 one newspaper, the *Christian Advocate*, testified to the city's thirst. It counted 573 places where liquor was sold, one for every sixty or so inhabitants. San Franciscans were swilling seven bottles of imported champagne to every one consumed in Boston. The gaming houses were packed from morning to morning. Josiah Royce wrote, with a mixture of sarcasm and fascination, that "Gambling in the big saloons, under the strangely brilliant lamplight, amid the wild music, the odd people, the sounding gold, used to be such a rapturous and fearful thing! One cannot express this odd rapture at all! Judges and clergymen used to elbow their way . . . to the tables and play with the rest. The men in San Francisco who did not thus gamble were too few to be noticed." Bawdy houses flourished likewise in a city of young men freed from Victorian constraint, flush with gold, or at least with dreams.

What Taylor called "an actual metropolis" boasting "street after street of well-built edifices" offered more than sin, of course. It was a city much too busy to stop and build little houses with picket fences, so hotels were numerous, if still struggling to meet eastern standards. And, in a cosmopolitan city of hungry young men, restaurants abounded. The *Annals* spoke of the "American dining rooms, the English lunch houses, the French cabarets, the Spanish fondas, the German wirtschafts, the Italian osterie, the Chinese chow-chows and so-on to the end of a very long chapter." Chic Delmonico's catered to whoever could afford its Parisian technicalities. Other favorites were the Poulet d'Or (soon transformed to the Poodle Dog

In 1934 the Emperor Norton was reburied at Woodlawn cemetery. Once again, the Pacific Union Club footed the bill. Mayor Angelo Rossi presided over the ceremony, which featured San Francisco's municipal band, a military salute, and the mournful playing of taps. Even today, when nothing else is cooking, a Norton festival will be mounted and the city's newspapers will again have cause to be grateful for the good copy the Emperor still generates.

by crusty Forty-Niners) and the Wigwam, noted for its hearty fare. By the late 1850s, food prices had dropped enough that 25–30 cents would buy an ample, uncomplicated meal.

It was a city of much more than eateries, smoky bars, posh bordellos and twenty-four-hour faro tables. From the beginning it was a great theater town. With the first Argonauts came minstrels and troubadors, and by mid-1849 they were turning people away from the tent flap when Rowe's Olympic Circus presented *Othello*. San Francisco was a mandatory stop for touring companies from Europe and the east. They might play the fabled Bella Union, or one of a series of Jenny Linds, named for the Swedish Nightingale.

One of the day's reigning celebrities who did appear in San Francisco was Lola Montez, "the international bad girl of the mid-Victorians," who arrived from Panama by side-wheeler in mid-1853. A reporter for the *Herald* wrote, "This distinguished wonder, this world-bewildering puzzle... has actually come to San Francisco, and her coming has acted like an application of fire to the combustible matter that creates public curiosity, excitement or *furore*." Montez was more notorious than talented, but her bodily and personal charms were more than sufficient, and when she performed her scandalous Spider Dance at the American Theater she satisfied all but the coldest spirits.

Manager J. Brutus Booth of the rival San Francisco Hall temporarily abandoned loftier fare (such as his family productions of Shakespeare) and satirized Montez in a skit entitled "The Actress of All Work." But San Francisco's favorite was dimpled, ringletted Lotta Crabtree. In the 1850s, when Lola Montez—at one time or another the wife of aristocrats and mistress of kings—was playing the odd and temporary role of a housewife in Grass Valley, she came across little Lotta, a precocious and eager talent. Under La Montez's guidance, Lotta learned the rudiments of show business and was soon the rage of San Francisco's music halls. Crabtree went on to become America's highest paid actress, but always counted San Francisco her home.

When she died in 1924 at the age of 77, Lotta gave away most of her $4 million fortune to a happy gallimaufry of worthy causes. One of her lesser, but most enduring bequests was the charmingly ugly "Lotta's Fountain," still to be found at the corner of Market and Kearny.

San Francisco in the 1850s probably had more college graduates than any other city in America. In those days a college degree carried the imputation of literary-mindedness, and San Francisco never lacked a robust life of letters. The city's physical and spiritual isolation created a hunger for news, both of home—wherever that might be—and of California. By 1853

The Wigwam has become the Tadich Grill ("the original cold-day restaurant," but that's another story...) located on California Street. Tadich's is officially one of California's 100 oldest businesses.

Jenny Lind never actually played San Francisco. One of the theaters named for her was bought by the city and converted into a City Hall. It sat across from Portsmouth Square in peaceful coexistence with one of the grandest gambling emporia, the El Dorado.

Opposite page
Portsmouth Square on the Fourth of July: 1850s "letter-sheets" like this impressed the folks back home with San Francisco's youthful energy and taste for celebration.

The "Actual Metropolis"

51

the city had twelve newspapers. Hubert Howe Bancroft estimated that over 1,000 Californians, most of them in San Francisco, were occupied in journalism in the 1850s. The most notable paper was the *Golden Era*, an eclectic literary-news journal with tiny type and large aspirations, founded in 1852 by Rollin Daggett and J. Macdonough Ford. It was in the *Golden Era* that Bret Harte first published his romantic short stories, and such western luminaries as William Rhodes and the old overlander turned litterateur Alonzo Delano limned a picture of the Golden State and its Queen City.

Gold Rush San Francisco was in many ways a "perpetual carnival." Men going to the diggings with high hopes, returning with gold or hard-won experience, energetic young men building a grand city. But there was a darker side beneath the glitter, one not much commented on but very real nonetheless.

The tents in which most San Franciscans still lived (and which, Taylor said, resembled "dwellings of solid light") were leaky, drafty, and cold. The streets, dusty one day and muddy the next, always crowded with traffic, were piled with rotting garbage. Cholera, pneumonia, and every kind of disease that thrives on unsanitary conditions were common.

For many, too, the sweet dream of gold had turned bitter. Impoverished, thousands of miles from home, left to the thin resources of charity, some succumbed to despair. Stephen Powers wrote, "This darling and sunny child of the republic is already as old as Europe in suicide."

Fire and Vigilantism: And some turned to crime. Money-mad San Francisco, well supplied with dark alleys and careless celebrants, was a cushy place for the criminal. "Have your pistol loaded and keep the middle of the street at night," warned Alonzo Delano. In August 1849, when the Gold Rush was turning his village into a metropolis, San Francisco's last *alcalde* and first mayor, John W. Geary, had warned his constituents, "You are without a single police officer or watchman and have not the means of confining a prisoner for an hour."

Revenue from land sales, liquor, and gambling licenses soon after enabled the city to patch together a rudimentary police force. But Albert Bernard de Russailh, for one, was unimpressed. "As for the police," he wrote, "I have only one thing to say. The police force is largely made up of ex-bandits and naturally the members are interested above all in saving their old friends from punishment."

There were lots of "old friends" about in the city. Many organized into bands, notably the infamous Sydney Ducks—English criminals escaping

John W. Geary, San Francisco's first mayor, was the donor of the land that later became Union Square, the heart of San Francisco, and had a major street named for him. He went on to become governor of Kansas, a Civil War officer, and, finally, governor of Pennsylvania.

banishment in Australia—and the similarly nefarious Hounds. The gangs swaggered through the streets and taverns of San Francisco, demanding protection money from cowed shopkeepers, taking advantage of what Josiah Royce called a "destructive general license [for] mischief-makers."

The Sydney Ducks, very active in the protection rackets, were popularly credited with setting at least some of the six major fires that burned through San Francisco with regularity from 1849 to 1851. The city was ridiculously susceptible to fire: wooden shanties built close together, a handy wind to stoke the blaze, and volunteer fire companies that were sometimes better at socializing than at putting out fires.

The Sydney Ducks and their ilk were not shy in threatening to take advantage of this tinderbox state of affairs. If a merchant fell behind in his protection payments, it was a simple matter to put his shop to the torch. If a few—or a few hundred—other buildings burned along with it, the Sydney Ducks and their fellow arsonists didn't much care.

The phoenix city: The fire of May 3–4, 1851, supposedly destroyed $20 million in property, but it hardly stopped the city's mad growth.

The "Actual Metropolis"

The fires of the 1840s and 50s inspired the city's official seal, with its heraldic "Phoenix issuing from flames." The great fire of 1906 was merely the latest in a city familiar with conflagrations. Though most of mid-nineteenth-century San Francisco has been demolished over the years, a surviving enclave can be seen at Jackson Square, near the Transamerica Pyramid.

The six great fires of those incendiary few years destroyed over three thousand buildings. San Francisco rebuilt itself after the fires with characteristically manic enthusiasm. After all, said the boosters, it gave the city a chance to get rid of those rickety shacks and tents and build some real (and perhaps fire-proof) buildings of brick, buildings with iron shutters and the air of permanency that befitted a real city. But if the wheels of progress refused to stop, so too did the ever-increasing lawlessness.

Whether or not they set any of the fires, the gangs were a bane on a city whose "conservative social elements" were trying to introduce order and respectability. The gangs were an anarchistic force, a threat not only to public safety but to the very existence of the city. For San Francisco to survive as more than an exotic and ephemeral boom town, they would have to be stopped.

One of the gangs' favorite targets was an encampment of Chileans on the slopes of Telegraph Hill. In July 1849 the Hounds raided "Little Chile," and arrogantly beat, raped, and plundered its inhabitants. The attack generated much outrage. A few Hounds were tried and, Josiah Royce related, "sentenced to long terms of imprisonment, which of course, were never inflicted on them," the authorities being so nearly impotent.

In early 1851, the city's criminals finally overplayed their hand. A merchant named C. J. Jansen was robbed and beaten in his store. It was hardly the first time such a thing had happened, but the city was in a restive mood. The *Alta* trembled with rage: "How many murders have been committed in this city within a year! And who has been hung or punished for it? Nobody. How many men shot and stabbed, knocked down and bruised; and who has been punished for it? How many thefts and arsons, robberies, and crimes of lesser note; and where are the perpetrators? Gentlemen at large, citizens free to reenact their outrages." Lynch fever was in contagion. "We deprecate lynch law," said the *Alta*, but who could tell what an outraged public might do to protect itself?

Typically, it was Sam Brannan—a man, Josiah Royce said, "always in love with shedding the blood of the wicked"—who began the counterattack. He stood atop soap boxes all over town bombasting against crime. It was time, Sam said, for law-abiding citizens to put an end to San Francisco's blatant and scary lawlessness, despite the "quibbles of the law, the insecurity of the prisons or the laxity of those who pretend to administer justice." In short order, a Committee of Vigilance, the archetype of all western vigilantes, was formed, with Brannan as president.

By June, the committee had worked itself into a retributive frenzy. The first unfortunate to attract its attention was a Sydney Duck named John

Jenkins, apprehended during an inept attempt to steal a safe. The vigilantes gave Jenkins a quick trial and hung him at Portsmouth Square on June 10. For 100 days, the vigilantes struck terror into the criminal heart. After another couple of necktie parties, uncounted Hounds and Ducks and unaffiliated malefactors laid low or slunk out of town, Sam Brannan's warnings ringing in their ears. A lid had been put on the city tempest. For a while.

Financial Decline: Lynch law is never a wonderful thing and the glee with which Sam Brannan and his cohorts shed the blood of the wicked may seem distasteful at far remove. But San Francisco was obeying a fundamental law when it protected itself against what were truly subversive elements.

There was a time, as historian Arthur Chandler has written, when "San Francisco had known life without a ruling class or castes—a privilege granted few other cities in the course of history." But that castelessness was largely the creation of the seemingly infinite river of riches flowing out of the Mother Lode. When that mad prosperity ended, when it was clear who had most of the chips at the end of the game, San Francisco became what its boosters had always wanted it to be: a near replica, with all its rough edges, of the settled and stratified cities of the east.

In 1853 the first great game, the time when every man sensed fortune in the next pan, the next deal of the cards, the next inbound ship, was ending. Placer gold was becoming scarce. More and more miners, older, perhaps wiser, were abandoning the Mother Lode, filtering into California's cities or, often rather sheepishly, going back home. They were being replaced by machinery, bought and operated by the growing capitalist class in California. But even the technology that replaced the rugged individualists of the old days was having trouble gnawing gold out of the foothills. In 1853 gold production dropped by $30 million. The Sierra would continue to give up its gold for years—to this day, when the price of gold is high enough, the hills are visited by panners, sluicers, and a few large companies taking a chance. But it was clear that the river of gold had dropped in its banks.

Immigration to the Golden State almost ceased. Merchants suddenly found themselves awash in goods ordered in the giddy days when the Gold Rush had seemed permanent. Money became scarce. Real estate values and rents dropped 20–30 percent, and by the end of 1854 it was reported that a third of the city's thousand stores were vacant. The depression reached its nadir when Page Bacon and Co., one of San Francisco's grandest banks, keeled over. San Francisco was never going to dry up like some penny-ante mining town, but it would be a while before it got over the shock of the end of the Gold Rush.

With the onset of hard times, the city's "marginals" began, as usual, to suffer, and some turned to crime. In fact, with the memory of the stern Committee of Vigilance fading, the new and fragile edifice of law and order seemed to be tottering. At mid-decade, the city was $2 million in debt, and some of its leading lights—such as Sam Brannan and James Lick—were refusing to pay their taxes.

In 1854 Henry Meiggs, called "Honest Harry," filched several hundred thousand dollars of the city's gold and sailed off to South America. Meiggs had been one of San Francisco's most high-pressured land speculators (his specialty was North Beach, then a boggy backwater, later the center of the Italian community). After he disappeared, it was discovered that he had been forging city warrants, papering the city with false wealth to hide his desperate overextension. It was assumed that he had been abetted by a negligent or downright corrupt city government. As the great Civil War general William Tecumseh Sherman, a San Francisco banker at the time, noted in his *Memoirs*, "politics had become a regular and profitable business." Confidence in the authorities, never very high, evaporated in the financial gloom.

The Second Committee of Vigilance: Flags of reform were unfurling everywhere. Crime was up, corruption widespread, and "the quibbles of the law" were standing in the way of real justice. Popular discontent found a champion in a gaunt, driven man named James King of William (so called to distinguish him from a horde of Kings). King of William was a bitter failed banker, a virulent antipapist and racist. But he was also a talented and tireless editor, and his newspaper, the *Evening Bulletin*, soon became the voice of the reformers.

The *Bulletin* raged against crime, prostitution, and civic corruption, but King of William had a favorite target in the person of James P. Casey, in 1856 a newly elected member of the city council. There was suspicion that Casey's election had been expedited by ballot-stuffing. The *Bulletin* was not shy in giving air to these suspicions, severely trying Casey's patience. When King of William published the fact that Casey had served time in New York's Sing Sing prison, Casey objected, and on May 14 shot him.

The crusading editor dallied dramatically on his deathbed for a week, but Casey was immediately arrested by vigilantes. A new Vigilance Committee was quickly formed under the leadership of William Tell Coleman, a 32-year-old veteran of the first committee five years before.

Within three days, 5,000 citizens had enlisted in the new vigilante corps. Enlisted is the word: the second committee was paramilitary, secretive, hierarchical. It established a well-guarded headquarters, Fort Gunnybags, near Portsmouth Square, and began patrolling the streets, establishing law and order. San Francisco's authorities, led by Mayor James Van Ness, put up a feeble show of defiance, and California Governor J. Neely Johnson tried to organize a militia under William Sherman's command to take the city back from the vigilantes. But, as Coleman told the Governor, "The people have no faith in the officers of the law."

On May 22, King of William having at last died, the committee flexed its muscles by hanging Casey and one of his cronies, a gambler named Charles Cora, who had killed a United States marshal. General Sherman—no friend of vigilantism—had to admit that the day of the executions was "exceedingly beautiful and the whole proceeding was orderly in the extreme," even though Cora and Casey were dispatched "without other trial than could be given in secret, and by night."

The first committee had been an improvised affair, but the second was fully prepared to replace the city's government for as long as necessary. Not everyone thought the coup a marvelous thing. Chief Justice Terry (this was before he shot Senator Broderick) called the vigilantes "damned pork merchants," and a "Law and Order" party was formed to uphold duly constituted authority. But when the city's leading newspaper, the *Herald*, was forced to close for questioning the committee's methods, most opponents kept nervously silent.

Young Prentice Mulford, newly arrived in town from Sag Harbor, later wrote, "San Francisco seemed to me then mostly fog in the morning, dust and wind in the afternoon, and Vigilance Committee the rest of the time." To the undesirables of San Francisco, the committee—grim-faced sons and brothers they were, marching about all day and night—must have seemed everywhere, all the time. The committee strung up four more criminals, deported a score, and put the fear of summary justice into countless others.

On July 18, 1856, the second Vigilance Committee staged a bombastic self-congratulatory parade as a prelude to ending its tenure. Congratulations were not entirely out of order. The committee could (and did, with typical volume) boast of having rid the city of its more noticeable class of criminal. It had also announced its resolve to keep a narrowed eye on civic affairs, which it did by forming a People's party that dominated San Francisco's politics until after the Civil War.

The graves of the executed Casey and Cora can be seen today in verdant Mission Dolores cemetery. Cora's faithful mistress Belle Ryan, who married him the night before he was hanged, is buried next to him. Their proximity is fitting—it was an insult to Belle's character that provoked Cora to shoot the marshal.

The "Actual Metropolis"

Coming of Age: By the end of the 1850s, San Francisco, despite its various tumults, was quieting down, stratifying, growing more mature. It had a population of well over 50,000, a growth in less than a decade which it had taken New York 190 years to accomplish, Boston 200, and Philadelphia 120. The city's "nabobs" had established themselves in grand houses on Rincon Hill (the leveled remains of which now lie beneath the maze of approaches to the Bay Bridge), the Irish were settling in the warm Mission District, and the area around Grant Avenue was already known as "Little China." The city's blacks—prohibited from voting, giving testimony against whites, even from riding in street cars—congregated in the area west of Montgomery Street and north of Jackson.

In 1859 Richard Henry Dana, proud to call himself "the veteran pioneer of all," came back to the Bay he had visited twenty-four years earlier. "I could scarcely keep my hold on reality at all," he wrote. Instead of the tiny hide and tallow trading center, graced only by Richardson's "shanty of rough boards," Dana saw a city of "well-built and well lighted streets." From his commodious room in the posh Oriental Hotel, he looked out over the city of San Francisco, "with its storehouses, towers and steeples; its courthouses, theaters, and hospitals; its daily journals; its well-filled learned professions; its fortresses and lighthouses; its wharves and harbor . . . the sole emporium of a new world, the awakened Pacific."

As actual a metropolis as it was becoming, San Francisco, with its polyglot population and its unique history, was never in any danger of becoming just another city. As Kevin Starr has written, "After the Gold Rush California would never lose a symbolic connection with the intensified pursuit of human happiness." For many decades to come, the capital of that pursuit was San Francisco.

But the city Dana saw was indisputably different, in size and structure and in spirit, from Gold Rush San Francisco. Already those early days had become the stuff of reminiscence and fable. Old Timers spoke with nostalgia of "the days when the water came up to Montgomery Street." And some of the bumptuous pioneers had become quiet burghers or, like Sam Brannan, only forty years old in 1859, victims of changing times.

Brannan had typified nascent San Francisco. He thought big, bought big, boosted, punished the wicked, and grew ever richer. But at the turn of the decade, Sam finally overreached himself when he bought a large tract of land in sylvan Napa County, 75 miles northeast of San Francisco. He intended to make the area's hot springs into a resort, the Saratoga of California, and so he called his dream Calistoga. Today's Calistoga is a charming spot and its curative waters and mud baths are a solace, but Calistoga was

Despite the endemic racism of the times, one of San Francisco's leading pioneers, William Leidesdorff, was a black Virgin Islander, who held the offices of city treasurer and chairman of the first public school board, and was U.S. vice-consul in Mexican Yerba Buena. Leidesdorff has a tiny street named for him in downtown San Francisco.

the beginning of the end for Sam Brannan.

His resort failed, and when land values in San Francisco fell, Brannan was suddenly overextended. The former Mormon took to drink, lost his money and his once towering confidence and drifted south. He died, impoverished, in Escondido in 1889. Like the man who found the gold, and the man who owned the land on which it was found, the man who began the Gold Rush ended his days in poverty.

Some might have seen a cautionary tale in Brannan's fate. They might have thought it signified that orderly growth had at last replaced the awesome confusion of the early days. But, as they often have in San Francisco's history, events swallowed reason; for in the next decade San Francisco would suddenly once again experience a fantastic burst of fortune.

At the end of the 1850s, on a particularly desolate part of the eastern slope of the Sierra, near pristine Lake Tahoe, a few placer miners were still eking out a hard-scrabble living, picking gold from the blue clay that oozed from the mountains. In the spring of 1859, that clay was identified as fabulously rich silver ore, and San Francisco once more became the world's great boom town.

The Bonanza Age

4

Some called the placer miners of the Virginia Range the "Old Californians" and some called them plain crazy. The Virginia Range (in what is now Washoe County, Nevada, midway between Carson City and Reno, about 170 miles from San Francisco) is a waste of hills and canyons and, as far as the Old Californians knew, a little gold, enough for an occasional "$10 gold rush," enough to keep them in whiskey and beans. They fried in the summer and spent the winter crowded into shacks, drinking, yarning, waiting for a visit from the legendary Snowshoe Thompson, who carried letters across the wintry Sierra and reminded the miners that the world still existed.

The real Gold Rush had passed them by, but since the early 1850s, the Washoe miners had been prying at the mountains, grubbing in the streams, melting snow to pan gravel and ooze high up on the slopes, trying to make their commitment pay off. Perhaps some mined from habit, like monks without a religion. And all the while they cursed the bluish clay that made extracting what gold there was so difficult. They were a little like James Marshall, who had simply been trying to build a sawmill on a river of gold. The denizens of the Virginia Range were simply trying to find gold on a mountain of silver.

They were not the brightest of men. The man who gave his name (and little else) to the richest mines on earth, Henry T. P. Comstock, was described by one historian as "loud-mouthed [and] half-mad," and by another as a "windy no-gooder." James "Old Virginny" Finney, who drunkenly christened the boom town of Virginia City after himself, was "picturesque, genial and open-handed," enough to give and fritter away claims that would have made him dizzily rich. Like the Spaniards of Alta California, little more than a decade before, the crusty tenants of the

Opposite page
Virginia City in 1861: "San Francisco's most solvent and essential suburb" was the clamorous center of the breathtakingly rich Comstock Lode.

Virginia Range would be driven from their land. It was only a matter of time before someone bothered to find out what that odd blue clay really was.

In June of 1859, a sample of the "blue stuff" was taken out of Sun Mountain, the center of the range, and sent down to Grass Valley to be assayed. Melville Atwood, the assayist, concluded that there was gold in there all right, but as the boys up in the Washoe knew too well, it was uphill work getting it out. Atwood also found, and this was the news that made history, $3876 of silver per ton of Sun Mountain ore.

News of the assay results quickly overflowed Grass Valley and spread across the state. Since Marshall's discovery eleven years earlier, there had been many false gold (and silver and what-have-you) rushes. In 1858, for instance, 23,000 grinning and ill-prepared men had set out for the Fraser River in British Columbia, only to return (those who could), frozen and goldless, a few months later. But experience is no match for hope, and in the summer of 1859, thousands of miners, merchants, speculators, and sharpies set aim for the mountains of Utah (soon to be Nevada) Territory. The Rush To Washoe was on. Before it was all over, perhaps a half billion dollars worth of silver would be dug out of those mountains.

It was like old times. San Francisco was sold out of pickaxes, pans, Levi Strauss pants, buckboards, salt pork, and all the accoutrements of mining life. One spectator wrote, "Our towns are near depleted . . . they look as languid as a consumptive girl. What has become of our sinewy and athletic fellow citizens? They are coursing through ravines and over mountaintops," looking for silver.

But the Silver Rush was not going to be a reprise of the old, already mythic "frontier democracy" of the Gold Rush, of young men panning and poking around with a knife in wooded foothills. That mucky blue clay needed expensive treatment to become silver. The Silver Rush would be a game for capitalists and engineers. But, in the summer of 1859, that remained to be seen. The first arrivals at the Comstock were optimism-drunk and rumor-fueled. They thought their millions were lying underfoot.

The Young Genius: Like the Gold Rush, the Comstock was endlessly fascinating and endlessly written about. One of the most entertaining accounts of life in the silver mecca was given by Mark Twain, whose book *Roughing It*, published in 1872, is a classic of straight-faced hyperbole and unblunted observation.

In mid-August 1861, 26-year-old Mark Twain arrived in Nevada with his brother Orion, who had been appointed secretary of the new Nevada

Territory by President Lincoln. The two had traveled by stage coach from St. Joseph, Missouri, the harrowing overland trek having been replaced by a relatively smooth twenty-day ride. But Twain had no trouble finding adventure along the way.

He collected tales of desperadoes, frontier justice, and the oddities of the Mormons, and he everywhere heard siren songs of wealth drifting eastward from the Comstock. Twain would always be a man with a talent for liking money. For a robust, clever young fellow like him, the Comstock seemed made to order. "I confess, without shame, that I expected to find masses of silver lying all about the ground," he wrote. "I was perfectly satisfied . . . that I was going to gather up, in a day or two, or at the furthest a week or two, silver enough to be satisfactorily wealthy—and so my fancy was already busy with plans for spending this money."

Like the rest of his fellow miners, Twain first had to do a little mining before he could enjoy his millions. As in the old days, miners stuck up claim notices on likely bits of mountainside, though what was likely and what wasn't was something of a mystery. The Argonauts had had handy streams doing much of their work for them, eroding the foothills and sending placer gold tumbling downstream. But the Comstock had few streams; instead the miners found miles of confounding hills and sagebrush. It was assumed that the mountains—Sun Mountain especially—were riddled with silver veins. The problem was finding them.

To keep a claim, a miner had to work it. But that often meant, Twain wrote, that miners "took up various claims and *commenced* shafts and tunnels on them but never finished any of them." Perhaps the labor involved in mining was unseemly to the Comstock's almost-millionaires. As Twain wrote:

> We prospected and took up new claims, put "notices" on them and gave them grandiloquent names. We traded some of our "feet" for "feet" in other people's claims. In a little while we owned largely in the "Gray Eagle," the "Columbiana," the "Branch Mint," the "Maria Jane," the "Universe," the "Root Hog Or Die," the "Samson and Delilah," the "Treasure Trove," the "Golconda," the "Sultana," the "Boomerang," the "Great Republic," the "Grand Mogul," and fifty other "mines" that had never been molested by a shovel or stratched with a pick. We had not less than thirty thousand "feet" apiece, in "the richest mines on earth" as the frenzied cant phrase had it—and were in debt to the butcher. We were stark mad with excitement—drunk with happiness—arrogantly compassionate toward the plodding millions who knew not our marvelous canyon—but our credit was not good at the grocer's.

Mark Twain was fleeing the Civil War, which was little more than a distant rumbling in California. As Franklin Walker, author of *San Francisco's Literary Frontier*, put it: "The war, which meant agony and destruction elsewhere, was an almost unmitigated blessing to the people living west of the Rockies, as it furthered home industry and built up population." More than 100,000 war-weary souls fled to California during the war. San Francisco was heavily pro-Union, however, and celebrated Union victories with speechifying and rallies—often led by the charismatic Unitarian minister Thomas Starr King—at what is now known as Union Square. Silver from the Comstock played a major role in financing the war effort, and California contributed $1 million, half the national total, to the Sanitary Fund, equivalent of the Red Cross.

It was the strangest phase of life one can imagine. It was a beggar's revel. There was nothing doing in the district—no mining—no milling—no productive effort—no income—and not enough money in the entire camp to buy a village lot in an Eastern village, hardly; and yet a stranger would have supposed he was talking among bloated millionaires.

That is Twain at his hyperbolic best. There was income and capital, and those mines were—soon—the richest on earth. The problem for Twain and the other bloated millionaires was that it was speculators and capitalists who were investing the capital and reaping the income.

Before long, most of the Old Californians and the sinewy, athletic fellows like Mark Twain had been bought out. H. T. P. Comstock might have been speaking for all of them when he wrote just before his death: "I am a regular born mountaineer, and did not know the intrigues of civilized rascality." Some of the most civilized rascals in the Comstock were lawyers taking advantage of the confusion over claims. As historian Grant H. Smith observed in *The History of the Comstock 1850–1920*, "The notices of location of the [early] Comstock mines were the crudest ever written . . . the confusion over titles was increased by erasures and mutilations in the record book which was kept on a shelf back of the bar of a saloon." Few miners were a match for clever lawyers or their clients.

When the claim book was moved out from behind the bar, the "beggar's revel" grew organized. Some of the early miners left the mountains, but many stayed. For, while it may not have been everyone's branch mint, the Comstock still tantalized with high wages, high excitement, and hope.

Virginia City: By the early 1860s the boom town of Virginia City—the Queen of the Comstock—was well established on the slopes of Sun Mountain. Many of the early miners had come to Virginia City, their illusions put aside for the moment, to work in the tunnels and foundries being built in, around, and under Sun Mountain.

After spending a year fortune hunting, Mark Twain too came to Virginia City. There young Twain found his trade, joining the sprightly *Territorial Enterprise* as a reporter. The newspaper and the town were an ideal training ground for a genius at wry exaggeration.

"Six months after my entry into journalism," Twain wrote, "the grand 'flush times' of silverland began [and] Virginia [City] grew to be the 'livest' town for its age and population that America had ever produced." Its fifteen or so thousand inhabitants "roosted royally midway up the steep side [of

The mines of Virginia City—the richest on earth—attracted the attention of some of the richest men on earth. The Rothschilds were much in evidence, and their local representative, Donald Davidson, gave his name to the great Comstock treasure chest, though traditionalists continued to call it Sun Mountain.

Former California chief justice and duelist David Terry, the killer of U.S. Senator David Broderick, was one of the lawyers who battened on the Comstock, which he hoped to convert into a Confederate colony.

Sun Mountain] seven thousand two hundred feet above the level of the sea." Beneath them were a maze of tunnels and a legion of miners busy gouging out the wealth of the Comstock. Twain got the nickname "The Washoe Giant" for telling stories like this one about the mining below Virginia City:

> In the middle of one of the principal business streets of Virginia, a man "located" a mining claim and began a shaft on it. He gave me a hundred feet of stock and I sold it for a fine suit of clothes because I was afraid somebody might fall down the shaft and sue for damages.

A. **Virginia City**
B. **Lake Tahoe**
C. **Modesto**

Plump with money lust and just plain lust, Virginia City boasted every artifact of a modern city, Twain wrote, including a full complement of politicians, "hurdy-gurdy houses . . . a dozen breweries . . . street fights, murders, inquests, riots . . . half a dozen jails and station houses in full operation and some talk of building a church."

J. Ross Browne saw it in a dimmer light. In a piece called "A Peep at Washoe," he wrote that Virginia City was "a mud hole; climate hurricanes and snow; water, a dilution of arsenic, plumbago and copperas; wood not at all except sagebrush . . . the mines are nothing more than squirrel holes on a large scale, the difference being that squirrels burrow in the ground because they live there and men because they want to live somewhere else."

It took a certain amount of effort to enjoy oneself amidst such desolation, but the men and women of Virginia City were up to it. San Francisco writer Warren Hinckle, in his ornately captivating book *The Richest Place on Earth*, called Virginia City a "twenty-four hour exercise in bacchanalia." Julia C. Bulette's celebrated house of negotiable virtue on D Street was equal to the best San Francisco itself had to offer. Chapman's Chop House on North B offered pismo clams and pisco punch around the clock. Day and night miners worked the gloomy shafts, day and night Virginia City's houses and streets shook from underground explosions, and day and night the foundries rang with the manufacture of wealth. And, keeping up with it all, winter and summer, frost and heat, day and night, were legions of saloons, bawdy houses, flop houses, and restaurants busily sating the unshy hungers of the miners.

In time, a certain air of refinement blew into town: a splendid opera house was built, richly furnished hotels sprang up to accommodate the capitalists inspecting their investments, and mine managers competed with each other to build fancy houses. But Virginia City never lost its rough edges—never could, what with arsenic-, plumbago- and copperas-ridden

When brothel-keeper Julia C. Bulette was murdered by a thief, the beloved madam was given a stately—if alcoholic—funeral by her "boys."

water, a climate of hurricanes and snow, and nary a tree to be seen in the whole precinct.

Though Virginia City became citified in its way, it was never the headquarters for its own riches. It was to San Francisco, with its banks and stock exchanges, that the Comstock money flowed. Three stages a day linked Virginia City with San Francisco and, Twain wrote, "the writhing serpent of dust" lifted up by pack-trains and mule teams "stretched unbroken from Virginia to California." As Lucius Beebe, the inimitable eccentric and chronicler of the Old West, noted, "Virginia City was San Francisco's most solvent and essential suburb."

By 1863, Mark Twain wrote, the "very blossom and culmination of the 'flush times'" had been reached. Almost $40 million had been taken out of Sun Mountain, and more than 2,000 mining companies were offering shares on the San Francisco exchanges. But as the silver was hunted deeper and deeper into the mountain, some major problems began to haunt the Comstock.

At about the 500-foot level, the shafts began flooding with near-boiling water. At that depth, ventilation for the miners (who were allotted 100 pounds of ice a day for cooling) became a great worry. And in many mines, the bonanza (Spanish for fair weather) was turning to *borrasca* (unprofitable rock). In 1864 many of those 2,000 mining companies collapsed. Many thought the Comstock was played out.

B illy Ralston: But a visionary San Francisco banker named William Chapman Ralston thought otherwise. Billy Ralston was one of San Francisco's most intriguing characters, a man who personified the silvery exuberance of late nineteenth-century San Francisco.

Ralston was a solid, handsome Scotch-Irishman who, like Mark Twain, had worked on Mississippi river boats in his youth. During the Gold Rush, he captained a steamship that bought Argonauts from Panama to the City of Gold. In the late 1850s, Ralston settled in San Francisco and became a banker. He was soon successful. As his friend Asbury Harpending wrote, Ralston combined "a marvelous head for business" with a "swift, off-hand fashion of saying pleasant things—not flatteries, but things that put a man in good humor with himself."

In 1864 Ralston opened the Bank of California at Battery and Washington Streets. The new bank's $3 million capitalization was a huge sum for the time, and all of it, the bank's announcement pointed out, was "paid-up cash in United States coin." The Bank of California was a partnership but, Julian Dana observed in *The Man Who Built San Francisco*, from the beginning "Billy

Lucius Beebe deserted New York's cafe society in 1950, and moved to Virginia City, then virtually a ghost town, where he revived the *Territorial Enterprise* and spent the next ten years composing, as his friend and admirer Warren Hinckle writes, "hydrophobic editorials" against modern life, "which he considered a 'street accident.'"

A Short History of San Francisco

Ralston *was* the Bank of California."

In the 1860s and 70s, Ralston, like Sam Brannan before him, was San Francisco's most conspicuous citizen. For all his tireless boosterism, though, he was a more complicated man than Sam. He had his melancholic moments and he had a charming streak of humility: once at a banquet in his honor it was proposed that a new agricultural community in the Central Valley be named for him. Ralston declined the honor. Such aggrandizement, he said forcefully, was not fitting. The next speaker suggested that the town be named in honor of Ralston's modesty. Hence the present-day city of Modesto.

Ralston was also a man, Harpending wrote, who had a "passionate, almost pathetic love of California. He wanted to see his state and city conspicuous throughout the world for enterprise and big things." Ralston bought and built on an imperial scale. His eighty-room mansion at Belmont, twenty miles south of the city, was a showplace, famous for its expansive gardens, its flock of servants (who had their own "Little Belmont" a half-mile away), its stables of redwood and mahogony inlaid with mother of pearl. Ralston financed theaters and opera houses and the prodigious Palace Hotel (though he died before it was completed). He invested in a bewildering variety of schemes, but it was the Comstock, above all, that filled Billy's and his bank's coffers.

Ralston was convinced that Sun Mountain was silvery still, and that modern technology and the Bank of California's capital could solve the Comstock's problems. In 1864 he hired a failed real estate speculator named William Sharon to manage the bank's interests in Nevada. Sharon, Julian Dana wrote, "was a little man with little black beady eyes, little mustache, and a ballooning ego." But Sharon was a cunning fellow, and he and Ralston soon found a way to grab control of the Comstock.

The struggling mining companies had been paying 3 to 5 percent interest a month on borrowed money. Ralston and Sharon offered loans at 2 percent and found eager takers. When the loans went into default, and most did, Ralston either foreclosed on the mines and took control or, just as effectively, took controlling stock as payment. Likewise, Ralston and Sharon brought up most of Virginia City's mills. What mines they didn't control were loath to oppose them, for without use of the mills, silver ore was just so much expensive rock. Within a few years, Ralston and Sharon and the Bank of California were the sovereigns of the Comstock.

The two bankers now set about making their gamble pay off. They inundated the Comstock with capital, installed bulky, expensive machinery to ventilate and drain the shafts, and hired engineers to devise new tunnel-

"The financial autocrat of the Pacific": William C. Ralston was San Francisco's all-time No. 1 mover and shaker.

One of William Ralston's less wise investments was in an ingenious scam called "The Great Diamond Hoax." In 1871 two confidence men convinced Ralston that they had found a rich diamond field in the Wyoming Territory. Ralston and favored friends invested heavily in the San Francisco and New York Mining and Commercial Company, only to find that the "Diamond Fields" had been salted with cheap stones (some of them already cut!). Ralston took his bath with characteristic good humor, buying up his fellow investors' worthless stock and framing the shares on his office walls.

ing methods. Some of the mines began to go back into bonanza. And so Ralston and Sharon coaxed the Comstock back to a measure of prosperity. Mining stocks were once again bought and sold feverishly, both in the exchanges and on street corners, where cheap issues were hawked like newspapers. Speculation mania was so epidemic that in the decade 1865–75 more money (or speculative money) was wrapped up in Comstock stocks than existed (in real form) on the whole Pacific Coast.

Billy Ralston and his Virginia City branch manager played the speculation game from a position of strength. And when some of the Bank of California's stockholders worried about the bank's deep commitment to the Comstock, Ralston replied, "I will personally guarantee the bank against loss." There was no turning back. Ralston bought up more mines, mills, stage lines, lumber companies, anything and everything to strengthen his stranglehold on the Comstock.

Sutro's Tunnel: Enter here Adolph Sutro, a cultured Prussian-born tobacco merchant and engineering genius. In February 1865 Sutro came to Billy Ralston with a plan to build a tunnel deep into Sun Mountain. The idea of such a tunnel may not have been Sutro's. But many, including Mark Twain, thought that Sutro was "one of the few men in the world who is gifted with the pluck and perseverence necessary to . . . hound such an undertaking to its completion." Sutro told Ralston what Twain told his readers: that "the Sutro Tunnel is to plow through the Comstock Lode from end to end, at a depth of two thousand feet, and then mining will be easy and comparatively inexpensive; and the momentous matters of drainage, and hoisting and hauling of ore will cease to be burdensome."

Sutro was a hard-working and dreaming man. "Although speaking broken English to the day of his death," wrote Grant Smith, "he was a fluent and convincing speaker and writer, and so quick and shifty in argument as to discomfort clever lawyers." He had already convinced the Nevada state legislature to grant him a right of way for his tunnel. From Billy Ralston he asked approval to sign royalty agreements with the individual mining companies. Ralston's mines were still plagued by drainage and ventilation problems. Sutro's tunnel promised to ease those problems and make access to and from the mines much simpler. Ralston was a friend of high purpose and ambition. He agreed to Sutro's request.

By the end of 1865, Sutro had signed agreements with twenty-three Comstock mines. Armed with a supportive letter from Ralston, he set out for the east coast to raise the $3 million he needed to begin the tunnel.

In July 1866 Congress passed the Sutro Tunnel Act, which gave Sutro federal right of way, liberal mining rights along the tunnel's seven-mile length, and a large plot of land at the tunnel's entrance. In New York, forty bankers agreed to loan Sutro his money, but on the condition that San Francisco money be raised first.

Back home again, Sutro persuaded Ralston to agree to a stock subscription by the mines that would meet with the New Yorkers' approval. But Adolph Sutro's weakness was vanity. He announced that his tunnel would henceforth be the jugular of the Comstock, and that before long "owls would roost in Virginia City." As Billy Ralston and his cohorts mulled over the federal law and Sutro's claims, they saw their monopoly fading away. And, if Sutro's fanfaronade weren't enough, there was the fact that he planned to name the city at the tunnel's mouth after himself. It would, Billy Ralston must have thought, be a long way from Modesto.

The Great Engineer: Adolph Sutro, tunneler, arborealist, Maecenas, and failed mayor.

The crucial stock subscriptions had been pledged subject to the consent of the mining companies—meaning the Ralston combine. In mid-1867 the companies blandly voted down the subscriptions, and Sutro began a frantic search for new money.

It took the deaths of thirty-seven miners at the Yellow Jacket Mine in April 1869 to save the tunnel. Sutro rushed to the scene of the accident, orated against the heartless owners, and convinced the miners that his tunnel would have prevented the tragedy. In a burst of solidarity, the miner's union pledged $50,000 for Sutro's company. Another loan by a London bank enabled him to at last begin his tunnel.

For years the mines of the Comstock and the stock exchanges and boardrooms of San Francisco quivered with arguments over the Great Engineer and his tunnel. In late 1869, the *Gold Hills News* called Sutro's tunnel "one of the most infamous and barefaced swindles ever put forth in Nevada." But to many miners and small stockholders in the tunnel, he was a humanitarian genius.

Sutro ran for the United States Senate in every election from 1872 to 1880, using his campaign to revile his enemies. He toured the country with lantern-slide lectures, drumming up money, and preaching the wonders of the tunnel. For nearly a decade, Sutro and his men gnawed through the mountains, until in the summer of 1878, the work was finished.

In October 1879, ex-president Ulysses S. Grant led a victory parade through the tunnel. At last mining would be "easy and comparatively inexpensive"; finally "the momentous matters of drainage and hoisting and hauling of ore [would] cease to be burdensome." It was a grand parade—but for the absence of Adolph Heinrich Joseph Sutro, who knew something the celebrants didn't. The tunnel had come too late. The Bonanza was over. Sutro had secretly sold his tunnel stock for a million dollars and retired to his mansion in San Francisco.

The Palace and the Park: While Adolph Sutro was still up in the Comstock building his tunnel, and the silver mines still seemed infinitely productive, Billy Ralston was in San Francisco savoring his prosperity. He was now, Asbury Harpending said, the "financial autocrat of the Pacific." His mines were hot and dangerous, but they were wonderfully lucrative. Not a day passed that a bullion-loaded mule train didn't come out of the mountains headed for the Bank of California's luxurious new headquarters at Sansome and California Streets.

His biographer, Julian Dana, wrote that "Ralston never asked the price of anything he bought from any merchant." He put that same disregard for quibbling to work in buying up, and into, portage and fur companies, railways, sugar refineries, furniture factories, watch companies, and the Spring Valley Water Company, San Francisco's major water supplier. In 1870 he began construction of his monument, the Palace Hotel, which was to take five years and $7 million to build.

Billy Ralston died two months before his hotel opened, but the Palace was a stupendous testimony to his energy and vision—probably the fanciest and most outlandish hostelry of its time. Though San Francisco had fewer than 150,000 inhabitants in 1870, the Palace was the largest urban hotel in America. It took up two and a half downtown acres, and boasted a bar tended by thirty men. As usual Ralston was both penny and pound foolish. He imported linen and marble, wood and china from all over the world. The posh eastern furniture company of W. & J. Sloane opened a San Francisco branch solely to furnish the mammoth hotel. Ralston lured Delmonico's chef to the Palace's kitchens, and ordered a gold dinner service for 100 (a setting of which can be seen in the Market Street lobby of the Palace's successor, the Sheraton Palace). From the street, the Palace presented a stately visage, with 7,000 bay windows looking out at the city. Internally, the hotel was dominated by a spectacular seven-story atrium, into which guests drove their carriages.

The Palace opened on October 15, 1875, with a gargantuan testimonial dinner for Lt. General Philip Sheridan ("the process of absorption went gaily forward until near midnight"). The *Morning Call*, for one, already thought it "the finest hotel on the face of the globe." Certainly the Palace the pinnacle of Western elegance and chest-thumping pride. It was a must-

W. & J. Sloane has remained in San Francisco ever since it opened a branch to supply Ralston's Palace Hotel, and still caters to the carriage trade from its Sutter Street store.

A Short History of San Francisco

see: the likes of Anthony Trollope, ex-president Grant, Rudyard Kipling (who refused to be unduly impressed), and Emperor Dom Pedro III of Brazil experienced its luxury.

True, there were some who thought the Palace a touch too much, seeing as it was never close to being filled. But Billy Ralston intended San Francisco to grow up to fit his hotel. He built the Palace to last, installing ultramodern fire-detection systems, and equipping the hotel with its own complex water supply. It was the embodiment of Billy Ralston's sterling ambition and large dreams. But, despite the best precautions money could buy, the Palace burned in the Fire of 1906.

Another of Ralston's many enthusiasms was the building of Golden Gate Park. San Francisco had been an almost instant city and during the Gold Rush had little time and less money to consider civic pleasantries like

The fine Irish linens of the Palace Hotel made up the deathbeds of a king and a president; King Kalakaua of Hawaii died there in 1891, and President Warren Harding died in the rebuilt Palace Hotel in 1923.

The Bonanza Age

parks. But, if it was going to become the Paris of the West, San Francisco had to be more than bustling commerce and elegant hotels. In the late 1860s, men like Ralston and Sam Brannan began planning for the future.

While San Francisco was building itself around the cove of Yerba Buena, the sandy north-western part of the Peninsula, called the "Outside Lands," had been largely ignored. There wasn't much out there except the Cliff House, which overlooked the Pacific in breezy isolation. The first of its several incarnations had been built in 1863, and soon had a reputation for raciness, but reaching the Cliff House meant a long and bumpy trip across the dunes.

The city's visionaries knew that San Francisco would eventually expand to the Pacific shore, and that before long speculators would begin buying up the Outside Lands. So, before all that acreage was gobbled up, a group of higher-minded citizens began lobbying for a great urban park. They were ridiculed and ignored (a park on sand dunes!) but they eventually had their way. In 1868 the Board of Supervisors accepted the California legislature's Order No. 800, which gave the city 1,000 acres of land in a rectilinear shape three miles long (beginning at Ocean Beach on the Pacific) and half a mile wide. Two years later, San Francisco's supervisors, with the sage advice of Frederick Law Olmsted, builder of New York's Central Park, chose a 24-year-old surveyor named Willam Hammond Hall to begin work on "the great white elephant," Golden Gate Park.

No one knew the Outside Lands better than William Hammond Hall, who had spent much of the Civil War surveying the Peninsula for the Union Army. Hall and his mentor Olmsted were convinced that the wasteland could be turned into a pleasant park. But their first problem was finding a plant to anchor the ever-shifting dunes, so that the grasses, shrubs, and trees that were to follow wouldn't be buried by blowing sand. Hall knew that native lupine would provide a strong anchor and base. But even the hardy lupine was quickly smothered.

The delightful story of Hall's eventual success is told by Harold Gilliam in his book *The Natural History of San Francisco*. It seems that a very frustrated Hall was one day camped near the present-day Chain of Lakes in the western part of the park. Hall fed his horse some barley, which had been accidently mixed with the ubiquitious sand. The horse refused the barley, and Hall threw it on the ground.

A few days later, he saw that the barley had taken root. He (or his horse) had at least solved the problem of the dunes. On top of the barley, Hall planted lupine, on top of the lupine, grasses, and so on up the botanical scale, until within a few years the Outside Lands had their first trees and

The state of California had title over San Francisco's "Outside Lands," and maintained nominal responsibility for Golden Gate Park until 1900.

The best place to see what the dunes of the "Outside Lands" looked like before Golden Gate Park was built is Fort Funston, just south of the Park. When conditions are right, it is also a good place to watch the almost miraculous flights of hang gliders.

the park began to blossom into one of the world's horticultural masterpieces.

With the sand conquered for the moment, Hall faced two other major problems. All that new greenery needed water, so he contracted with Billy Ralston's Spring Valley Water Company for 100,000 gallons a day. This was barely enough to keep things blooming, but by 1885 wells sunk deep into the sand gave the park an ample water supply. In the early 1900s, two water-pumping windmills were built near Ocean Beach to take advantage of the steady westerly winds and supplied the park with 70,000 gallons of water per hour.

Hall's second and most crucial problem was keeping new sand from being blown inland from Ocean Beach, as it had been for so many centuries. If nature had its way, then and now, half of San Francisco would eventually revert to rolling sand dunes, and the homes of the western part of the city and Golden Gate Park would be silently covered. Hall solved the problem by having a six- to ten-foot-high sea-wall built along the ocean front. That wall, now buried beneath the Great Highway, effectively halted the millennial sand flow.

By the late 1870s, Golden Gate Park had become one of San Francisco's most cherished assets. Its 150,000 trees shaded picnickers, its two miles of gently curving roadway were thronged by carriages and happy idlers on Sunday outings. But William Hammond Hall had no time to rest on his plush green lawns beneath some elegant Monterey cypress. Instead, he kept a tireless vigilance against those who didn't share his vision of an untrammeled urban nature preserve and sought to chip away at the park. Hall was a proud man, whose imperious ways put him in conflict with the Park Commission, some of whose members were aligned with land developers. Billy Ralston used his influence to protect Hall, but when Ralston died in 1875, Hall was plagued by vindictive investigations. He was charged with various malfeasances, including the soft-headed claim that he was cutting down park trees for his own use. In 1876 Hall had enough and resigned. With Hall gone, the Park Commission adopted a tight, small-souled budget. The Park was far from complete, but in the years following Hall's resignation, little new planting was done. Then, in July 1890 the colossus of Golden Gate Park, a crusty Scotsman named John McLaren ascended to the superintendent's post.

McLaren combined an almost mystical love of nature with a brigadier's passion for orderliness and command. He was a student of William Hall, and, like him, loathed the gimcracks and geegaws forever being foisted on the Park. If McLaren was overruled and forced to accept a statue of a politician or someone's favorite composer, he usually manged to hide it behind

The second of the two windmills in Golden Gate Park, the Murphy, was supposedly the largest in the world; these charming oddities are being reconditioned today.

One of Park surveyor William Hammond Hall's most troublesome detractors was powerful W.W. Stow, the Union Pacific railroad's political agent in Sacramento. Hall called the handsome artificial lake named after Stow "a shoestring tied around a watermelon" (the watermelon being Strawberry Hill, the highest point in the Park). After his resignation as Park superintendent, Hall went on to become California's first state engineer. He died, aged eighty-eight, in 1934.

foliage; he wanted the Park to be a place of refuge, as nearly natural as possible. It was a place to be *used*, and so he especially forbade "Keep Off the Grass" signs.

"Uncle John" McLaren served as Golden Gate Park's benign dictator until his death, at the age of ninety-three, in 1943. His devotion to the Park was total: asked on his ninetieth birthday what he wanted as a present, he replied, "Ten thousand pounds of good manure." He fended off generations of developers, and courted and admonished the city's politicians, few of whom could stand up to his wrath.

During McLaren's fifty-three years as superintendent, Golden Gate Park remained happily free of needless development and ornamentation, and it has remained so, arguably, to this day. But in 1894 McLaren's patience was tried by the first of San Francisco's three big fairs, the California Midwinter International Exposition, the brainchild of the San Francisco *Chronicle*'s cofounder, M.H. de Young, who wanted to acquaint the world with the subtle glories of the city's winter climate. With a newspaperman's promotional zeal, and the shared enthusiasm of the town's movers and shakers, de Young (who had been vice-president of the 1893 Chicago Columbian Exposition and was anything but a slow learner) cranked up a gaudy, delightful exposition.

To McLaren's dismay, a 200-acre parcel in the heart of the Park was cleared and 100 temporary buildings built to entertain and edify the masses, 2.5 million of whom attended during the exposition's six-month life. When the exposition closed, in July 1894, McLaren eagerly tore down almost all the buildings and set to replanting the site. But a few vestiges of the grand celebration of turn-of-the-century vitality still exist: the Music Concourse, the De Young Museum (rebuilt in 1917), and the popular Japanese Tea Garden.

The Railroad: While Golden Gate Park was still a gleam in William Hammond Hall's eyes, his defender Billy Ralston was madly buying real estate and building supplies, getting ready for a deluge of prosperity. In the late 1860s Ralston, and just about every San Francisco moneyman, was convinced that the long-awaited completion of the transcontinental railway would be the capstone to San Francisco's greatness. It must have seemed a remarkable progression: the Gold Rush in 1849, the Silver Rush in 1859, and in 1869 the linking of the coasts and the expected invasion of immigrants, factories, and new money.

Plans for a transcontinental railroad had been floating around for years. But during the 1850s the railroad, like much else, became entangled

San Francisco's winter months are rainy, and less than hot. But how many other places turn green in winter?

The Japanese Tea Garden was lovingly maintained and operated by the Hagiwara family from 1895 to World War II, when the family and 93,000 other Californians of Japanese ancestry were summarily "relocated" to concentration camps in the state's hinterlands. The Hagiwara family's devotion to the Tea Garden was unrecognized until 1974, when a bronze memorial was dedicated to them. Though the plaque doesn't mention it, Makato Hagiwara invented the "fortune cookie" here. Around the turn of the century, the idea caught on with the city's Chinese restaurants, and the rest is history, of a sort.

A Short History of San Francisco

in the bitter North-South controversy. Voluminous surveys had concluded that a line to California was equally feasible through northern or southern states. The North opposed a southern route because it might further slavery (among other things) and the South saw a northern route as adding to the North's economic dominance. It took the outbreak of the Civil War in 1861 to end the debate. Mineral-rich California and Nevada were too valuable to be left so dangerously isolated: the Federal government wanted the railroad and it wanted it fast.

In the winter of 1862 Congress voted the Pacific Railroad Act, which gave extremely low-interest financing, generous subsidies, and vast amounts of land along the right of way to two rail companies, the Union Pacific, building from Omaha, and the Central Pacific, building from Sacramento. The genius of the Central Pacific was a young engineer named Theodore Dehone Judah, who had built California's first railroad, the twenty-two-mile Sacramento Valley line, in 1856. For years Judah had been roaming the Sierra, surveying a rail route across the escarpment. But his plans and enthusiasm failed to ignite San Francisco's capitalists. In 1861 Judah turned to a group of Sacramento merchants and businessmen, who in June formed the Central Pacific Railroad.

Four uncommonly crafty members of the Sacramento combine—Mark Hopkins, Leland Stanford, Collis Huntington, and Charles Crocker—were quick to realize the stupendous potential of their investment. They bought up and squeezed out their fellow investors, including Judah (who fought to regain control of his railroad until his death from Yellow Fever in 1863). The Big Four, as the sagacious ex-merchants came to be called, had captured a rolling gold mine. The federal government's haste to get the railroad built meant that not only did Huntington, Stanford et al. build the line with ridiculously cheap borrowed money, but ended up owning vast tracts of rich western land in a checkerboard pattern on either side of the right of way. The four grew preposterously rich, moved to San Francisco, and began a mansion-building competition on Nob Hill. They treated the Central Pacific (which became the Southern Pacific in 1884) like a private money preserve. In the last four months of 1877, for example, the Big Four made the following personal withdrawals from the company's overstuffed treasury: Crocker $31,000, Huntington $57,000, Stanford $276,000, but parsimonious Hopkins a mere $800. In time, the Southern Pacific became a colossus, owner of virtually all the state's transportation companies, 9,000 miles of track and, even today, four million acres of wooded, fertile, or mineral-rich land. Known as "The Octopus," the Southern Pacific and its owners utterly dominated California politics for decades.

Financial Bust: San Francisco waited gleefully as the Central Pacific and the Union Pacific inched towards each other. In April 1868, five years and three months after construction had begun at Front Street in Sacramento, the first Central Pacific train breached the Sierra at Theodore Judah's carefully chosen Donner Pass. (The crossing of the mountains had been a monumental and hair-raising bit of engineering; from then on the going was relatively easy.) Thirteen months later, on May 12, 1869, a thousand or so people met at Promontory Point, Utah, "to enact the last scene of a mighty drama of peace, on a little grassy plain surrounded by green-clad hills, with the snow-clad summits of the Wasatch Mountains looking down," as the *Alta California*'s correspondent wrote. At the joining of the rails, a Golden Spike was driven, speeches made, trains whistled, and the coasts were linked.

San Francisco greeted the news with characteristic revels. The bars were jammed, the streets crowded, and some citizens carried a banner reading "San Francisco Annexes the United States." More soberly, the *Evening Bulletin* editorialized, "It would be folly to say that quick communication will not stimulate trade." That's what they all thought—Billy Ralston, James Lick, William Sharon, the Big Four, all of them. San Francisco's isolation had been irksome. With the completion of the railway, the city could now chug to the forefront of American cities.

But an obscure writer and raging theorist named Henry George knew better. George predicted in the *Overland Monthly* that the expected boom would fail to materialize. He understood that San Francisco had profited in many ways from its seclusion at the continent's edge. In effect, it had been protected by a tariff of plains, desert, and mountains from the mighty factories of the east. Now those factories, George saw, would be able to flood the west with cheap manufactured goods. George saw, too, that the thousands of Chinese brought to California to work on the railroad (they were called "Crocker's Pets") were soon going to occupy stage center in a terrible racist drama.

George's predictions were astonishingly accurate. The boom was a will-o'-the-wisp, blown through the minds of overheated boosters, men drunk on their own hopes. Eastern manufacturers did flood the San Francisco market. Immigration increased somewhat, but most of the newcomers were unable to find work. Real estate dealings of $3.5 million in 1869 had fallen $1.5 million a year later. San Francisco was suddenly, unexpectedly plunged into a financial depression.

Troubles piled up: a severe drought in 1869–70 crippled the state's agricultural industry. In 1871 San Francisco's stock exchange dealings, chronically overstimulated by silver stock speculation, fell from $80 million to $20 million in less than a week. A last ironic indignity was the fact, conveniently overlooked before, that the transcontinental railway's western terminus was in Sacramento (later in much-looked-down-upon Oakland). Thus San Francisco suddenly lost its position as the queenly crossroads of trade to and from the west.

Ralston's Defeat: For William Chapman Ralston the failure of the railroad to bring prosperity was a calamity. And, if it weren't enough that his investments in building materials (for the boom that never came) and real estate (likewise) had brutally overextended him and the Bank of California, his primacy over the Comstock had been shattered in 1874, when the Consolidated Virginia Mine exploded into the biggest bonanza of all.

The Consolidated Virginia, one of a score of middling-productive mines in the Comstock, was owned by a quartet of coarse-grained sons of Eire named James Flood, William O'Brien, James Fair, and John W. Mackay, the fabled "Bonanza Kings."

Flood and O'Brien had owned the Auction Lunch Saloon in San Francisco, a tavern frequented by mining stock speculators, and the two publicans parlayed a sharp ear for inside information into a measure of success as mining stock speculators themselves. Fair and Mackay were old mining men, working away in the Comstock waiting for their main chance. In 1872 the four got together and bought the Consolidated Virginia for a mere $80,000. Two years later, it suddenly became the most prolific producer of silver in the Comstock's well-feathered history. In one month in 1876, the Con Virginia poured out $6 million in ore. For years, it produced millions monthly, making the Bonanza Kings supremely rich in the process.

They had come a long way, Mackay especially. He had arrived in Virginia City in 1859. Just before he reached town, he grandly threw away his last four bits. His equally impoverished partner asked why. "So we can arrive like gentlemen," answered Mackay. Once, in Virginia City, he told his friend, "All I want is $30,000, with that I can make my old mother happy." Grant Smith relates that when Mackay's income from the Con Virginia "was $300,000 a month [his partner] twitted him about the remark, to which Mackay responded with his slow smile: 'W-well, I've ch-changed my mind.'"

The Bonanza Kings quickly moved to San Francisco and joined the other nobs on their hill. They also formed the Nevada Bank of California—the most heavily capitalized bank of its day.

William Sharon, who later became a United States Senator from Nevada, cheated Ralston even after the latter's death. As executor of Ralston's estate, he shortchanged his associate's family, and ended up owner of the Palace Hotel and Ralston's beloved Belmont estate.

Panic: The Bank of California shuts its doors.

By this time Ralson was in trouble up to his diamond stickpin; he had spent and borrowed himself and the Bank of California into a mire of debt. Ralston gambled that his Ophir mine would pull him out. But behind his back William Sharon was quietly and deftly selling Ophir stock, driving down its price. Before he had time to catch on to his former colleague's euchring, Ralston was left with parcels of useless stock.

On "Black Friday," August 26, 1875, the inevitable finally happened. Nervous depositors made a run on the Bank of California. Such panics weren't rare in a town where financial news and gossip were as common as fog. And as he and his fellow bankers had done in the past, Billy Ralston

A Short History of San Francisco

tried to calm the mob at Sansome and California Streets with bravado and showy confidence.

But it was too late. The bank was forced to close. When it re-opened, chastened and wary, five weeks later, Billy Ralston was already part of history. The day after the bank shut its massive oaken doors, Ralston resigned. While taking his customary afternoon swim near Meigg's Wharf that day, he drowned.

Ralston was reportedly $5 million in debt. His once towering reputation had been shattered. So it was no surprise that he was generally assumed to have committed suicide. That was surely what William Sharon must have been thinking when he laconically commented, "Best thing he could have done."

Ralston's death was a national sensation, "what the Lizzie Borden murders were to be a few years later," according to Lucius Beebe. But, even had he lived, had his power clung to him, Billy Ralston would have been fairly powerless in the face of the troubles now descending on San Francisco.

The Gilded Age

5

Once the San Francisco worker had been a prince among men. "Here Labor controls Capital," James Collier, the port collector, wrote in 1849. During the Gold Rush, when everyone else was gallivanting around the foothills trying to get rich, an able-bodied worker expected a lordly "ounce"—$16—for a day's work. There were times when the city paused in its mad growth, but with all the fires, the almost constant building and rebuilding, the steady immigration, the riverine silver money from the Comstock, and the building of the railroad, the San Francisco workingman had always been needed, respected, and, in the context of those rough times, well treated.

But the completion of the transcontinental railroad changed all that. Billy Ralston and the others had scoffed and bought building materials and real estate, but as Henry George had predicted the young factories of San Francisco were swamped by eastern competition newly freed from wartime work.

In the ensuing depression, thousands were suddenly without work. Angry and disillusioned (in the land, the very city of opportunity), many of the men looked for a scapegoat. As time cleared their heads a little, the city's workingmen did begin to see the real cause of their troubles. But at first they—many of them at least—gave in to the old temptation of racism. The industrious Chinese, used to living on a fraction of what the white workers needed, were a handy explanation for economic discomfort. Henry George had predicted that too.

Since the Gold Rush, the Chinese had usually been accepted as a harmless, exotic minority. They were routinely denied most civil liberties, but they weren't the rebellious sort (it seemed anyway). They congregated in their busy ghetto of Chinatown and by the 1870s had slowly, through hard work and brilliant organization, established virtual monopolies in cigar

Opposite page
America's only rolling landmark: This 2nd Street two-unit car and dummy is little different from the surviving Hyde and California Street cable cars.

The Gilded Age

making and the garment industry, and held strong positions in boot and brick making among other enterprises.

When 10,000 or so of "Crocker's Pets" were left out of work following the completion of the railroad, many came to San Francisco. When the unemployed white San Franciscan looked around, he increasingly saw Chinese: working in the cigar factories, the brick factories, the Chinatown sweatshops, in white-owned businesses of all kinds. In 1872 Chinese held half of San Francisco's factory jobs. They were willing to work longer, perhaps harder; they were certainly willing to work for less.

And so, many San Franciscans began to blame the Chinese for unemployment and depression. In 1875 a "Workingman's Slate" took power at City Hall. The new administration passed a series of vindictive anti-Chinese ordinances, most of which were too petty to be taken seriously and were soon ignored or forgotten. But the election of such racists served to give a kind of informal approval to the plague of anti-Chinese feeling that took hold of San Francisco.

The word "hoodlum" was coined in late-nineteenth-century San Francisco to describe the city's roving youth gangs.

The Chinese were easy prey for the city's hoodlums. Beatings were random, frequent, and rarely punished. Mark Twain wrote scathingly of the way the Chinese were treated: "He is a great convenience to everybody—even the worst class of white men, for he bears the most of their sins, suffering fines for their petty thefts, imprisonment for their robberies, and death for their murders. Any white man can swear a Chinaman's life away in the courts, but no Chinaman can testify against a white man."

Not only couldn't the Chinese testify, they couldn't own land, couldn't apply for citizenship, and had their symbolic queues cut off in jail (the infamous Pigtail Ordinance). The Board of Supervisors even forbade the use of Chinese granite on public buildings.

"No California *gentleman* or *lady* ever abuses or oppresses a Chinaman," wrote Mark Twain, "only the scum of the population do it . . . and habitually and consistently the policemen and politician likewise, for these are the dust-licking pimps and slaves of the scum, there as elsewhere in America." Twain's spleen was merrily boiling, as usual, but he hardly exaggerated the hatred shown the "Celestials."

In the summer of 1877, resentment exploded into mob action. On July 23 rioters burned, beat, and wrecked their way through Chinatown. Two days later, they did it again. But the patience of the ladies and gentlemen of the city's solid middle class was at an end. William Tell Coleman, leader of the Vigilance Committee of 1856, was recruited (from what must have seemed even then the fog of antiquity) to head a "Committee of Safety." Coleman's brigade soon numbered more than five thousand defenders of law, order, and property (for the rioters had not been scrupulous in confining their activities to Chinatown). With a psychological boost from two warships anchored at Benicia and 1,200 soldiers ready in the Presidio, the committee stopped the roving mobs.

But conditions remained grim for the unemployed, and the presence of the city's 46,000 Chinese still rankled. In sandlots and dingy theaters around town, angry workingmen searched for organization and answers. The sandlotters found a leader in a deep-lunged orator named Dennis Kearney. Ironically, Kearney had been a member of Coleman's Committee of Safety, as befitted a small businessman. But when his drayage business failed, Kearney joined the Teamsters Union, became a sandlot activist and, in time, helped form the influential and radical Workingmen's party of California.

Kearney and his followers went beyond puerile racism (though "The Chinese Must Go!" remained their rallying cry). They ranted at the impacted wealth and privilege of the monopolists, they raved against the mining kings and railroad moguls and their servants in government. And the most persuasive raver of all was Dennis Kearney, "The Cicero of the Sandlots."

The sandlotters paraded around the city, flexing their muscles, shouting slogans, scaring the Chinese and denouncing what Kearney called the "rich hell-hounds of California." One of their greatest demonstrations was in the fall of 1877, when 3,000 men marched up Nob Hill to give witness against Charles Crocker's famous "spite fence."

To many, the spite fence was a perfect example of the powerlessness of the common man, in this case an undertaker named Nicholas Yung. Yung had bought a sliver of the Nob Hill lot bounded by Jones, Taylor, Sacramento, and California before the hill became a millionaire's preserve. When Crocker bought the rest of the lot and built his early Renaissance mansion, he offered to buy Yung out. The stubborn undertaker refused. Crocker—not at all used to defiance—then built a forty-foot, threesided fence around Yung's house, which made living in it like living at the bottom of a deep well.

The spite fence was high civic entertainment, the subject of cartoons and innumerable dance-hall jokes. But to the sandlotters it was distinctly unfunny. To them, the spite fence was a measure of the appalling inequalities of wealth in a city once known for its frontier democracy. While thousands of men kept barely alive by wit and private charity, the millionaires ate off their gold plates. The *Morning Call* reported in 1871 that a mere 121 San Franciscans controlled $146 million in private wealth. And amidst or under all that were the thousands of unemployed.

"If I give the order to hang Crocker," Kearney said in front of the railroad man's mansion that autumn day, "It will be done." The sandlotters demanded that the spite fence be torn down within thirty days and walked back down the hill, visions of millionaires cowering behind locked doors dancing in their heads.

But the fence remained standing and things didn't much improve for the workingmen of San Francisco. Dennis Kearney though, became a national celebrity. He traveled far and wide espousing his populist creed. For, though the Workingmen's party was still stained with racism, it was well ahead of its time in calling for direct election of United State Senators, compulsory education, state regulation of banks, railroads, and industry, and, since "eight hours is sufficient day's work for any man the law should make it so."

In mid-1877 the Workingmen's party reached its zenith. It achieved control over a much-needed California Constitutional Convention. But the convention did little more (by way of reform) than enact various high-minded (and a few low-minded, anti-Chinese) laws, most of which proved ineffective. The party was soon torn by internal feuding. Kearney was charged with this, that, and the other scandalous misbehavior and was forced to resign. In another of the turnarounds which marked his career (and that of many American radicals), he thereupon reenlisted in the bourgeoisie, becoming a prosperous and conservative commodities speculator until his death at sixty in 1907.

The Workingmen's party was spunky and quite often had the right idea, but in the end it was powerless against the economic facts of the late 1870s. There were no strong unions to protect the workingman against discount labor, nothing could stop yet another drought in 1876, the playing-out of gold and silver couldn't be postponed, and little could be done about the fantastic amounts of sorely needed capital tied up in what Mark Twain called "the gambling carnival" of stock speculation, a carnival that ended suddenly at the end of the decade, leaving thousands dazed and penniless.

Good Times in Bad: San Francisco has always been a city buffeted by the unexpected. But even in the worst of times it scarcely lets up in its "intensified pursuit of human happiness." So, in its years of economic decline, following the disappointment of the railway, and in the decades following, when it regained its monetary muscle and strode confidently toward a new century, San Francisco kept right on polishing its reputation for excitement and devotion to life's finer things.

"The climate of California deals kindly with excess," wrote visiting

Rudyard Kipling. He found San Francisco "a mad city, inhabited for the most part by perfectly insane people whose women are of a remarkable beauty." San Francisco society had a "captivating rush and whirl. Recklessness is in the air."

This was the age of the free lunch, when, wrote Kipling, "You paid for a drink and you got as much as you wanted to eat . . . for something under a rupee a day a man can feed himself sumptuously even though he be bankrupt." All evidence points to quite a few who spent more than a rupee. "The native pours his vanity into himself at unholy hours," Kipling wrote. "Drinking is more than an institution, it is a religion."

If drinking was a religion, there was ample opportunity for the faithful to practice. From the fabulous Palace Bar, with its troop of solicitous tenders, to the surreal Cobweb Palace on Meigg's Wharf, where a patron might share his drink with a half-tame monkey, the town housed an amazing number and variety of taverns and eateries.

San Franciscans thronged to Maye's Oyster House for eastern oysters and fresh fish (and still do). "Lucky" Baldwin's Hotel at Powell and Market, with its $25,000 lobby clock and its posh dining room, was a rival of the Palace. Less fancy was the What Cheer House, a gustatory celebration of the American virtues of simplicity and quantity. The Fior D'Italia was (and still is) a favorite of the Italian community, and Jack's on Sacramento has been serving hearty repasts since 1864. In not a few of San Francisco's restaurants, the well-heeled diner could retire upstairs with a bottle of vintage bubbly and perhaps enjoy a high-stakes poker game or the company of a delightful young lady "from the finest eastern finishing school."

At night, Kearny Street was a genteel thoroughfare of light and color, its restaurants and bars filled, its pavement delicately trodden by the ladies who so impressed Rudyard Kipling. Barely out of sight of Kearny Street's "large-boned, deep-chested, delicate-handed women, and long, elastic, well-built boys"—San Francisco's middle classes—was Morton Street (now chaste Maiden Lane), an alley of cut-rate depravity ruled by one Iodoform Kate.

On weekends, San Franciscans visited one of the city's many beerhalls, took refreshment and admired the seals from the Cliff House, or made family outings to the new park. A favorite of all ages was spectacular Woodward's Gardens, a pre-Disneyland extravaganza of gardens, exotic animals, rides, and uplifting art exhibits, owned by the What Cheer House's Robert Woodward. Woodward's Gardens, located at Mission and 14th Street, was a San Francisco landmark until 1883. Its charms were immortalized by poet Robert Frost, who had honed his imagination there as a San Francisco lad in the early 1880s.

Rudyard Kipling was well used to the exotic, coming as he did from India, but San Francisco widened his eyes even so. He found it exciting, if rather crude. One special disappointment was hearing his beloved Bret Harte read in an American accent, which he called "the language of thieves." "Get an American lady to read you 'How Santa Claus came to Simpson's Bar,' and see how much is, under her tongue, left of the beauty of the original," he lamented.

San Francisco's appetite for theater continued in high style. Maguire's Opera House and "Lucky" Baldwin's presented the flower of the American theater, from Adah Isaacs Menken (world-famous for her performance in *Mazeppa*, in which, clad only in tights, she was carried off-stage by a black stallion), to Sarah Bernhardt, and, as the years passed, the likes of Harry Houdini, Marie Dressler, and the Barrymores. David Belasco, the greatest producer and dramatist of his day, learned his art in the raucous music halls of Virginia City and at Maguire's and Baldwin's posh Academy of Music, located next to "Lucky's" Market Street hotel.

Like David Belasco, Robert Frost is only one of a number of native luminaries not usually associated with San Francisco. Others include James J. Corbett, who vanquished John L. Sullivan in 1892; Isadora Duncan; Rube Goldberg; Alice B. Toklas; Lincoln Steffens; and the tireless war-wager Robert Strange McNamara.

Victorians and Cable Cars: It was during this period—from the 1870s to the turn of the century—that most of San Francisco's marvelous Victorian houses were built. These stylish buildings, so forcefully nostalgic, are a living part of San Francisco's charm. Most of the Victorians were built of redwood, which is unique to the Pacific Coast of California and Oregon. Redwood was plentiful in those days and had the added virtue of being easily worked. It had to be, for this was an era confident enough to relish decoration, and the Victorians, with their dentils, cartouches, spindles, finials, festoons, arches, and, above all, their bay windows, were products of a hearty aesthetic confidence.

These old houses seem wonderfully individualistic to us today, but many of them were built in tracts by such companies as the Real Estate Associates, alone responsible for building more than 1,000 houses in the 1870s. Many of the Victorians were identical, or were collections of towers and balusters, frills and foundations ordered from a thick catalogue. As hand-crafted as the Victorians now appear, they were once criticized for their uniformity. Today there is a widespread movement to rehabilitate the Victorians and—less traditionally but nonetheless entertainingly—paint them in unique rainbow colors. They maintain a pleasant dignity somehow lacking in the mass-produced stucco homes built in the Sunset and southern parts of the city following World War II (though it is easy to forget that those new houses provided thousands of families with relatively cheap, well-built housing just when it was needed most).

The Victorians were products of a steady rise in San Francisco's population in the years 1870–1900. From just under 150,000 people in 1870, the city grew to 342,000 at the end of the nineteenth century. At the beginning of that thirty-year period, San Francisco was still the child of Yerba Buena Cove; almost all its buildings occupied the northeast quadrant of the upper Peninsula. By 1900 the city had moved out to embrace Golden Gate

A Short History of San Francisco

Park, settled the Outside Lands, and begun to move southward. The growing city moved upward, too, climbing the hills that had been the aeries of a hardy few.

The final conquest of San Francisco's hills and the city's energetic spread were helped along, sometimes made possible, by the invention of another San Francisco trademark, the cable car. The city's first public transport, a horse-drawn omnibus, began operating in 1850, carrying passengers, produce, chickens, and pigs from Portsmouth Square to Mission Dolores. By the 1870s, at least six transportation companies were operating. But all the people, lumber, masonry, and raw materials of the fledgling city had to be carried in horse-drawn cars and carts. Even the dutiful horses of the day found the city's steep hills, stamped with the up-and-down grid patterns of the early days, tough going.

In 1870 a London-born Scotsman named Andrew Hallidie arrived in San Francisco. Since coming to California during the Gold Rush, Hallidie had been a pioneer in the manufacture of steel cable for the mines of the west. In 1869, after witnessing a gruesome street car accident caused by a broken-down horse trying to climb a slippery street, Hallidie began cogitating a plan to use his cable to replace the hapless and inefficient horse-teams. For three years he theorized and tinkered, until in 1873 he perfected his invention: an endless cable, running in a slot just below street level, kept in motion by gigantic wheels housed in "barns." The car's gripman fastened onto the running cable to move and disengaged (and braked!) to stop.

On August 2, 1873, Hallidie unveiled the Clay Street Railroad Company's first cable car. What seems so quaint to us was high technology in those days and the crowd at Kearny and Clay was free with its huzzahs as the car, trailing its 12-seat dummy, hippled up Clay Street. Hallidie's cable cars were a booming success. The city's steepest hills were safely attainable. By 1890 San Francisco had eight cable car companies, operating 600 cars over 100 miles of track. The idea caught on all over America, as well as in Sydney and London.

As motorcars and electric lines appeared, the cable cars were made obsolete—everywhere, that is, but in San Francisco, where they became a civic symbol and the source of endless television commercials. In 1964 San Francisco's beloved cable cars were designated the nation's only mobile historical landmark. There are only three lines operating today, but despite their inefficiency, their tendency to bewilder traffic, the vast sums required to keep them moving, and the not overpublicized fact that safety is not foremost among their virtues, the cable cars are today as much a part of San Francisco as fog and sourdough bread.

A. Nob Hill
B. Russian Hill
C. Telegraph Hill
D. Twin Peaks
E. Mount Davidson

The last of San Francisco's cable car "barns" can be seen, still amiably functioning, at Washington and Mason Streets.

Millionaires and Mansions: Typically, among the first to benefit from the cable cars were San Francisco's bumper crop of millionaires. In 1878 a group of the city's Croesuses, led by Leland Stanford, joined forces to build their own line, the California Street Cable Car Railroad, which ran handily from the financial district to the crest of Nob Hill (and continued westward down the hill, opening up the Western Addition to more plebian development).

When the likes of Nicholas Yung and other stouthearted folk had lived on those heights, it had been called the California Street Hill. Now that cable cars provided sturdy and regular access to the hilltop, the nabobs moved in, and the California Street Hill became Nob Hill, the city's most elegant address. With their plutocratic beachhead secured, the millionaires began a mansion-building jamboree, competing in size, opulence, and often in giddy lack of taste.

James Ben Ali Haggin, a lawyer and mine owner, opened up the sweepstakes with a sixty-room manse on Taylor Street. Haggin was a horse-fancier, and constructed a hilltop stable so splendidly furnished, Lucius Beebe later reported, that "Haggin had a number of guests in for supper with the horses after the Opera the last evening before the fire of 1906 and the footmen were still clearing the table at five in the morning when the crack of doom sounded."

William Sharon's mansion had the first hydraulic elevator in the west and Beebe (who had a good eye for such florid excess) wrote that "the drapes, curtains and lambrequins cost $2,000 for every window in the house." Charles Crocker's house cost him $2.3 million (not including, presumably, the spite fence). Willis Polk, an innovative and acerbic architect, called the mansion the "delirium of a wood carver," but the interior was graced by a million dollars' worth of paintings, including Millet's *The Sower*, ordered by the former dry-goods clerk.

Crocker's Southern Pacific partner Mark Hopkins countered with a $3 million effort generally considered the pinnacle of awkward eclecticism. Mrs. Hopkins is usually blamed for the crypto-elegant forced fusion of styles, fantasies, and what may have been an architect driven loony by his client. The summit of Nob Hill was crowned by old saloon-keeper James Flood's brownstone mansion, surrounded by a $50,000 bronze fence "reminiscent of a bar rail."

Today only Flood's home remains in testimony to Nob Hill's Age of Excess. The Bonanza King's manse—the only one to escape the 1906 fire— now houses the Pacific Union Club. In addition to the hotels named for Huntington, Stanford, and Hopkins, there is the Fairmont, built by James

Two major Nob Hill hotels, the Mark Hopkins and the Stanford Court, now occupy the sites of the mansions built by their namesakes. Huntington's house was in what is now Huntington Park, across California Street from the hotel named after him, and the Crocker family gave the site of Charles Crocker's mansion for the building of Grace Cathedral. Crocker Bank is one of America's largest. Though the Big Four did not distinguish themselves as philanthropists, Leland Stanford did create one of the nation's great universities in memory of a son who died at fifteen in 1884.

Stanford University, located south of San Francisco in Palo Alto, was ruled with crotchety devotion by Mrs. Stanford after the railroad mogul's death in 1893. It is well worth a visit, if only for its architecture, especially the bombastic piety of the chapel.

Atop Nob Hill: When Charles Crocker built his California Street mansion (the gingerbready one behind David Colton's white wedding cake), he put up a 40-foot "spite fence" around stubborn Nicholas Yung's modest dwelling.

Fair's daughter in 1906. It barely survived the catastrophe of '06 and opened in 1907. A marble portico called the Portals of the Past—all that the fire left of the Towne mansion—today stands in melancholy isolation, another reminder of the glory that was, beside Golden Gate Park's Lloyd Lake.

The Written Word: The palaces and peculations of the rich were a favorite topic for San Francisco's four intensely competitive newspapers, the *Call*, the *Bulletin* (James King of William's old paper), the *Chronicle*, and the *Examiner*.

In the late 1880s and 1890s, the *Examiner*—self-styled "The Monarch of the Dailies"—was bursting with energy under the leadership of its owner William Randolph Hearst. Young Hearst had been given the paper as a present by his father George, an early Comstock mogul. The *Examiner* served as a laboratory for the shocking, successful methods Hearst would later bring to New York and the rest of America, methods that became known as Yellow Journalism. Hearst later became a reactionary, but in his early days the *Examiner* was the only pro-union paper in town.

Equipped with a dazzling bank account and boundless nerve, Hearst freely looted his competitors of talent and flattered his writers with high wages. Among the *Examiner*'s stars was the splendidly vitriolic Ambrose Bierce, famous for his *Devil's Dictionary*, which defined happiness as "an agreeable sensation arising from the misery of another." Jack London covered the Russo-Japanese War for the *Examiner* and, on a lighter note, Ernest Thayer's *Casey at the Bat* first appeared in Hearst's brainchild.

The *Chronicle* was no less lively. Begun by the brothers Charles and M.H. de Young on a $20 grubstake from their landlord, it was originally a theater sheet. In time the *Chronicle* became a feisty, crusading newspaper in the western tradition. In fact, one of the brothers paid the ultimate price for his paper's aggressive opinions. In 1880 Charles de Young was shot dead by the son of Mayor Isaac Kalloch, a Workingmen's party candidate who was a favorite *Chronicle* target. (De Young had himself wounded the elder Kalloch earlier, so the argument may not have been entirely political.) Five years later, the surviving brother, M.H. de Young, was nearly killed by Adolph Spreckels, who objected to the *Chronicle*'s attacks on the Spreckels sugar clan.

San Francisco—populated by an unusually well-educated if unsoaped bunch of Argonauts—had enjoyed a robust literary life since the founding of the *Golden Era* in 1852. The *Golden Era* was hungrily read throughout the west; its four pages were filled with a melange: clippings from the eastern press, classic poems, the musings of housewife philosophers, and the sentiment-

While the *Call* and the *Bulletin* faded from the scene in 1929 and 1965 respectively, the *San Francisco Chronicle* today has the largest circulation in Northern California. The afternoon *Examiner* faltered in the 1960s and 70s but is rebuilding under aggressive leadership. The two papers share advertising departments and copublish a Sunday edition.

drenched efforts of miner-poets.

The *Golden Era* started Bret Harte on his way and published the already celebrated "Washoe Giant," Mark Twain. It nursed such talents as shy young Prentice Mulford, flamboyant Cincinnatus Hiner Miller (better known as Joaquin Miller, after California's legendary bandit Joaquin Murieta) and first published a reserved poet named Ina Donna Coolbrith, who later became the doyenne of San Francisco's belles lettres and, as an Oakland city librarian, nudged young Jack London toward the literary life.

As the *Golden Era* began to lose steam in the late 1860s, the *Overland Monthly* took its place as the west's outstanding literary journal. Unlike the *Golden Era*, the *Overland Monthly* published only original material. Henry George delivered his prophecies of financial ruin in its first issue. Clarence King, the explorer, climber, and tall-tale artist (and debunker of the Diamond Hoax) was a contributor, as was Charles Warren Stoddard, a delicate truth-seeker who sparked Robert Louis Stevenson's interest in the South Seas.

Bret Harte (who also served as the *Overland Monthly*'s editor for three years) hit his stride in the colorful short stories that did so much to create the romantic myth of the Gold Rush. Harte's stories were teary, but he was no cynic: when told that a reader had wept over one of his stories, Harte replied, "Well, he had a right to. I wept when I wrote it."

The *Overland Monthly* flourished until 1875. In 1883 it was resurrected with a fair amount of success (and continued publishing until 1935). But it had lost much of its early vim, and Ambrose Bierce typically buried it with mockery, calling it the "Warmed-Over Monthly."

By 1875 over 150 books had been produced by California authors. Most were factual treatises on mining, geography, and the like, but many were pure "literature," evidence of California's allure.

Part of San Francisco's charm lay in its extreme isolation and the hot-house atmosphere that came from the collected energies of so many gifted, adventurous people. Living in San Francisco was like living on the edge of the universe (albeit with ample creature comforts), and reports from the frontier were eagerly read back east. But, with the coming of the railroad, some of San Francisco's remote charm disappeared. When travel to the west became a simple matter of buying a ticket and settling into a damask seat for a few days, many of San Francisco's authors left to try their talents in the east and in Europe.

Bret Harte left in 1872. Mark Twain had left a few years earlier (and never returned to the land he later said had given him the most joyous years of his life). Prentice Mulford went to England, as did Joaquin Miller, who, dressed in buckskins, wearing his blond hair shoulder length, created a sensation by cleverly acting the role of the precocious frontiersman. But Miller was more than a mere posturer, and he achieved great popular and critical success with his *Songs of the Sierras*, and later with *My Life among the Modocs*, a largely apocryphal account of his hair-raising adventures with the Northern California Indians.

One of Joaquin Miller's favorite stunts was to contrive outlandish compliments to the beauties of the day. He once poured rose petals over the greatest of them, Lily Langtry.

With the departure of its best talent, San Francisco's literary life entered a fallow period that lasted until the turn of the century, when a new generation of writers and poets such as George Sterling, Jack London, and the great realist novelist Frank Norris came of age.

George, Bancroft, and Muir: Throughout the blustery 1870s, Henry George was at work on what was to become a classic of late nineteenth-century radical economics. Since arriving in San Francisco in 1857, George had seen a good deal of progress in the west and, sadly, not a little poverty. There was his own: he worked for years at whatever jobs he could find, finally managing to squeeze a living out of writing and editing. And then there was the poverty that progress itself seemed to bring.

In 1868 George had foreseen the economic calamity of the transcontinental railroad. During the next decade, he mulled over more subtle problems and inequities. He gorged on economic theory with the zeal of the self-taught, writing and thinking far into the night, trying to find the solution to the dismal problem of economic disparity in a land of plenty. In 1879 he published *Progress and Poverty*, a book which the great English socialist Sidney Webb later praised as "the event which more than any other stimulated the revival of socialism in Great Britain." In *Progress and Poverty* George synthesized his experience as a miner and a nosey newspaperman in real estate mad San Francisco. He argued that the root cause of economic inequity was the ownership of land and the ability of landowners to raise rents with increases in productivity. He proposed a single tax which would tax land at 100 percent of its rental value, ending speculation and freeing progress from the grip of landowners.

It was, and still is, an audacious notion, and over the years not a few cities and even counties have toyed with the idea of the single tax (though it has never been implemented). In any case, *Progress and Poverty* became a national bestseller. Freed from his own poverty, Henry George set out on the lecture trail. He attracted a zealous constituency and was nearly elected mayor of New York in 1887. Until his death in 1897, George was a leading figure in economic thought, a crusader against the laissez-faire of the day.

If Henry George was kept on his way by demon idealism, another large figure in San Francisco's literary landscape, glowingly successful Hubert Howe Bancroft, was quite at home in the marketplace. Bancroft had arrived in San Francisco in 1852. After making a fortune as a stationer and bookseller, he built a five-story building on Market Street in 1869. The first four floors housed his business, but the fifth, the famous "workshop"—a kind of literary sweatshop, really—was reserved for Bancroft's platoons of writers and researchers, busily creating his dream, the encyclopedic *History of the West*. There Bancroft's workers labored ten hours a day, six days a week. They wrote outlines, sent out queries, conducted interviews, and cross-referenced the matchless collection of western books, pamphlets, and maps Bancroft had amassed over the years. The enterprise was a teeming pyramid, with Hubert Howe Bancroft at the top; though he barely dipped his pen in the ocean of ink his works consumed, his was the only name to grace the title pages of the thirty-nine volumes the history factory eventually produced. It was a gargantuan undertaking, covering the indigenous western peoples, the histories of Mexico, Central America, and the western states and, the centerpiece of Bancroft's opus, seven volumes of California history. Franklin Walker called it the "greatest feat of historiography since Thucydides."

From a purely literary standpoint, Bancroft's works have not exactly blossomed with time. Their scholarship was sometimes flawed (as in the seven fawning volumes of the *Chronicles of the Builders*) and the writing is often cranky and tedious. But the *History of the West* was a noble task. Bancroft's books brought the drama of western history to thousands. Even more importantly, he compiled and conserved a vast trove of material that might otherwise have been lost.

Though he invested nearly a half-million dollars in his thirty-year project, Bancroft was no dreamer. His books were sold by well-coached, aggressive salesmen. They were offered on a subscription basis, with various bindings and financing available, just sign here ma'am. Bancroft was a child of his enterprising age. Not many, before or since, have made such a fortune on the dry stuff of history.

And then there was John Muir, the patron saint of America's conservationists. Unlike George, Muir was little interested in politics, and even less in the Bancroftian pursuit of worldly goods. But in time his influence was a match for theirs—greater perhaps, as it is growing still.

In 1868, 30-year-old, Scottish-born John Muir left his home in Wisconsin. He had already undertaken long treks—once from Indiana to the Gulf of Mexico—and knew how to get by with few comforts. Setting out for California, Muir took with him only a knapsack, a journal (inscribed

In 1905 Hubert Howe Bancroft sold his 50,000-book library to the University of California. Some were critical of the $250,000 price, and even of the collection's worth, so Bancroft anted up $100,000 of it himself. But today's Bancroft Library is perhaps the greatest library of western history in the world.

"John Muir, Earth-planet, Universe") and an open spirit. After a thousand-mile walk, Muir arrived in California. He sampled San Francisco life for a short time and then confidently set out across the Central Valley for the great gleaming canyon of the Yosemite.

John Muir spent six years in the incomparably gorgeous Yosemite, working at a hostelry owned by a sympathetic fellow writer named James Hutchings (who had published *Hutching's Magazine* from 1856–61). But for the most part he tramped the wilderness of the Sierra Nevada, the "Range of Light," as he called it. He made brave and historic climbs on the range's clean white granite, explored its ribbony waterfalls, and contemplated the nature and origins of the unique cliffs of the Yosemite. Through intuition, reading, and pure blue-sky inspiration, Muir became expert in botany, zoology, and geology.

He was the first to recognize that Yosemite's precipices had been carved by glaciers. His theories clashed with those of the experts of the day, who looked upon him as an eccentric mystic. One of his most cocksure critics was Josiah Whitney, leader of California's first extensive survey (for whom the state's, and outside Alaska, the country's highest mountain, is named). Whitney was a marvelous explorer, but he lacked Muir's rich vein of intuitive genius.

Muir's sensitive yet direct writings, first published in *Harper's Magazine*, and later collected in numerous books, excited thousands of readers. For years he traveled throughout the west and Alaska, studying glaciers, climbing mountains, building the experience that made him one of America's great plain-talking philosophers.

In later years, Muir settled down somewhat as a farmer near Martinez in the Bay Area. But his influence was constantly and widely felt: in the creation of Yosemite National Park in 1890, in his election as the first president of the Sierra Club two years later, and in the creation of the National Forest System, in many ways the product of his friendship with presidents Grover Cleveland and Teddy Roosevelt, with whom Muir used to discuss conservation over Yosemite campfires. More than any other man or woman, he opened the eyes of America to California and the west's natural treasures, and helped form a resolve to protect that heritage.

John Muir was seventy-six when he died in 1914—living long enough to join in the debate as to whether automobiles should be allowed in Yosemite Park. Naturally, Muir thought that they should be banned, but he was overruled. Today the magnificent valley has a smog problem, and the National Park Service is hunting for ways to cut down auto use.

The Sirocco of Sin: When the Sierra Club was founded in 1892, it numbered among its members some of San Francisco's most prominent citizens. By that time, it had become fashionable for the powerful to dabble in good causes and burnish their reputations for probity.

For some, a little image-polishing was a priority. San Francisco in the 1880s and 1890s was a city in which civic virtue was as rare as a snowstorm.

Among the many things the railroad had brought to San Francisco was the eastern bacillus of political bossism. From the beginning, San Francisco's politics had never suffered from undue concern with honesty or the sanctity of the ballot box. Its first election in 1848—and just about every one after—was mud-spattered. But chicanery and corruption had usually been rather informal, an "Honest Harry" Meiggs running off with city money or a city councilman shooting an editor.

The city's first mentor in well-organized corruption was Irish-born Christopher Buckley, a pupil of New York's Tammany Hall, who had alighted in San Francisco in the mid-1870s. "Blind Chris" (the victim of bad whiskey, it was said—though his mental powers were certainly unimpaired), bought the Snug Cafe, conveniently a few doors down from the "temporary" city offices at Washington and Kearny Streets. Buckley soon put his Tammany Hall lessons to work. He gained control of the city's Democratic party and by the 1880s virtually ruled San Francisco politics.

"Blind Chris" was a blithely, entertainingly cynical sort: in state matters he usually hewed close to the Southern Pacific line and used the railroad's monetary blandishments to buy the loyalty of an army of hacks, corrupt cops, judges, and city officials. He ran San Francisco like a giant, scenic protection racket. The city was enjoying a prosperous lull, and its respectable elements were for the most part content to ignore the indecencies that lurked out of sight of Nob Hill and the new Victorian row houses. Much of Buckley's power came from kickbacks and bribery. But he and his machine also fattened on protection money offered up by the gamblers, pimps, and gangsters of the city's two ulcers of depravity, Chinatown and the Barbary Coast.

Before Buckley began milking it of protection money, Chinatown had been left to follow its own impenetrable ways. In order to infiltrate the ghetto, Buckley formed an alliance with the famous Fung Jing Toy, known as "Little Pete." While "Little Pete" presided over Chinatown's day-to-day corruption, Buckley was content to keep the authorities out and, like some distant emperor, receive kow-tow. Buckley needed a Chinese partner, for few Westerners could speak Chinese and fewer understood the loyalties and feuds of what was in many ways a foreign country nestled in the city's heart.

San Francisco's 50,000 or so Chinese, hounded by hoodlums, prejudice, and exclusionary laws everywhere but in their exotic enclave, were governed by district organizations called the Six Companies. The Six Companies, powerful to this day, were originally responsible for the "importation" and regulation of workers from China. Later they became the chief force of law

A new city hall was begun at Polk and MacAllister Streets in 1871. The building was to be the largest and most breath-taking of its kind in America, but as construction extended beyond the planned two years to five, ten, and fifteen years, and costs rose from $1 million to $5 million to $8 million, the building became known as "The New City Hall Ruin." Finally completed in 1900, it lasted until 1906, when the earthquake turned it into an authentic ruin.

and order in Chinatown and in all the state's Chinese communities.

Chinatown was a great tourist attraction, then as now. Its narrow streets, thronged with black-robed, pigtailed folk, its famous bejeweled mandarins, passing haughtily through the rush, its—to Western senses—odd foods, its otherworldly sounds and smells, were like a trip to the Orient. For the very adventurous, there were the notorious opium dens (twenty-six were counted in 1885), sources of unending stories in the nation's scandal sheets. But beneath the titillation and curiosity of the whites—and the hard-working, law-abiding character of most Chinese—was the rotten underside of Chinatown life.

Vice in Chinatown was controlled by the infamous "tongs," notably Little Pete's Sue Yop Tong. The word tong simply means "association," but to the newspaper readers of the day it came to signify the blood-chilling aspects of Chinese life. In the oddly genteel Chinese way, the tongs hid behind innocuous names. One called itself the On Leong Society, which means "the Chamber of Tranquil Conscientiousness." The On Leong was one of Chinatown's chief traffickers in slave girls.

The tongs and their cowed minions controlled Chinatown's hideously dingy sweatshops and inhuman "cribs." They propagated drug-slavery and extorted tribute from the quarter's shopkeepers, always aided by the indifference of the city's white majority and a city government controlled by "The Blind White Devil."

As ghastly as it was, Chinatown had no monopoly on immorality. Equally degraded was the Barbary Coast, a notorious hive of gambling hells, bordellos, and seedy taverns centered around Pacific Avenue near the waterfront. It was on the Barbary Coast that unwary sailors and civilians might be served the proverbial Mickey Finn and shanghaied (a word supposed to have originated in San Francisco), or an unsuspecting maiden (or semblance thereof) could be sold into white slavery. In *Lights and Shades of San Francisco*, B. E. Lloyd described the world-famous theme park of sin that was the Barbary Coast:

> The villains of every nationality held high carnival there... It was a grand theater of crime. The glittering stiletto, the long bowie knife, the bottle containing the deadly drug and the audacious navy revolver, were much used implements in the plays that were there enacted... licentiousness, debauchery, pollution, loathsome disease, insanity from dissipation, misery, poverty, wealth, profanity, blasphemy and death are there. And Hell, yawning to receive the putrid mass is there.

Sailors, crooks, and unwise tourists from every global cranny packed the Moro, the Thunderbolt, the Dew-Drop-In. "Nymphes du pave" haunted the dark alleyways of Bull Run, Moketown, and Murder Point.

The panjandrums of what the *Chronicle* called "the coast on which no gentle breezes blow" were known as "Rangers"—street toughs and enforcers. The Rangers, pimps, and saloon keepers of the Barbary Coast had little to fear from the law if they kept their protection payments up and cultivated the right city father. To Chris Buckley, the Barbary Coast was another source of revenue, and as long as the tide of prosperity swirled about San Francisco in the 1880s and 1890s, straighter citizens were fairly content to avert their gaze from the "wild sirocco of sin."

By the 1880s California had settled down enough to build a solid base of prosperity. The state was the world's leading wheat producer. Advanced

Besides "hoodlum" and "shanghai," San Francisco has provided the language with a number of neologisms. According to an article in the *Examiner* (April 8, 1979), these include: "malarkey" (a local, large-talking fellow), "sandlot" (the best place to hold a rally), "beatnik" (invented by Herb Caen, the city's columnist laureate) and "Levi's" (for old Mr. Strauss, the pants maker).

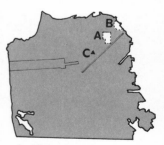

A. Chinatown
B. Barbary Coast
C. City Hall

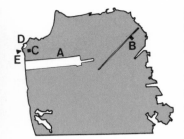

A. Golden Gate Park
B. Palace Hotel
C. Sutro Mansion
D. Sutro Baths
E. Cliff House

gold-mining methods were producing a steady stream of wealth (compared to the torrent of earlier years) and California's industries were at last competing with the east.

San Francisco was by far the largest city in the state—one in four Californians lived there until the turn of the century—and the city was still the crossroads of western wealth. In 1890 it was the eighth largest American city and was second only to New York in foreign trade. But San Francisco was by now tightly bound to the national economy, and when the great depression of 1893 struck, it suffered along with the rest of the country. Five hundred and eighteen banks failed nationwide, eighteen of them in San Francisco.

There wasn't much the city could do about a national depression. But civic corruption, which had been palatable during more prosperous times, once more became a smoking issue. Buckley had been tolerated in part because he had kept taxes down, but his penny-pinching had led to the deterioration of the city's buildings; streets were potholed, parks in decay, and government inefficient at best. San Francisco's newspapers, especially Hearst's *Examiner*, began once more to beat the drums of reform.

The Reformists: In 1891 Christopher Buckley was removed as head of the Democractic party and fled the state just ahead of an indictment (he died, full of years and ill-gotten gains in Vallejo in 1922). A reformist Popular party gathered itself together amid the city's political ruins and persuaded 65-year-old Adolph Sutro to run for mayor.

After the hurried sale of his Comstock properties (a little-known scandal in San Francisco), Sutro had returned to the city and had become a philanthropic grandee. He bought up a vast acreage—one-twelfth of the city's total area—and launched an ambitious tree-planting program; the eucalyptus forest of Mt. Sutro (then Mt. Parnassus) was just one of the many treeless areas planted by Sutro and the troops of schoolchildren he enlisted. Installed in a mansion overlooking the Cliff House (which he owned) and the fabulous Sutro Baths (which he owned and had conceived), Sutro busied himself with his massive library and his charities. He had kept clear of political finagling, and seemed to the gentlemenly reformers an ideal mayoral candidate.

Sutro was duly elected in 1894. But the man some still called the Great Engineer was used to exercising a benign autocracy. He was ill-suited to the compromises and Byzantine workings of government. Sutro's single term was a disappointment all around, especially to himself. He ruefully admitted, "I could not manage politicians." He died during the summer of

1898, his once sterling reputation sadly tarnished.

In 1897 the reformers found a promising mayoral candidate in James Duval Phelan, the 36-year-old scion of a wealthy banking family. Phelan was Jesuit-educated, cultured, and widely traveled. As a second-generation San Franciscan, secure in wealth and removed from the rough and tumble of the frontier, he was free to spend his energies on something besides the pursuit of money. As Kevin Starr has written, Phelan "related to San Francisco in the manner of a Renaissance Prince." So the old city of frontier democracy turned in a time of need to an aristocrat, albeit one newly minted.

Phelan was elected and served for five years. He oversaw the passage of a much-needed new city charter, aided and encouraged the arts, supported a revitalized park system, helped bring the mishmash of municipal transport systems under city ownership, and, in all, brought a refreshing respectability to civic affairs. But Phelan's sense of noblesse oblige really wasn't well suited to a city still, and always, made up of less refined, often bitterly opposed factions.

On the one hand there were the capitalists of the public-be-damned school and their natural allies, the small businessmen of San Francisco. On the other there were the workingmen, now gathering together in unions, demanding a piece of the pie, or in the case of the more radical—and there were not a few of those—the whole pie.

In 1901 the newly strong unions began a series of strikes. On April 19 the United Railroad Employees struck. On May 1 the restaurant workers went out; three weeks later, they were joined by the International Association of Machinists. When the vital teamsters struck in late July, the city was nearing a crisis. The business community countered by forming the Employers Alliance, which claimed to see unionism as a plot to bring down the whole structure of society. The strikers were little more than greedy communists, went the reactionary refrain, echoed in all the city's newspapers save the *Examiner*. The Employers Alliance upped the ante by threatening harsh boycotts against any businessman who caved in to the strikers. At the end of July, 13,000 members of the City Front Association—an umbrella group that included the maritime and longshoremen's unions—joined the strike. The battle lines were well and truly drawn, and in the middle of it all stood well-meaning, moderate James Phelan.

By September the city was at a standstill. Twenty thousand workers were idle, and 200 ships lay in the harbor. Rioting, fights, threats, and sabotage were widespread. On October 2, California Governor Henry T. Gage threatened to send in the National Guard if the impasse continued. Gage's threat was effective. Negotiations began and were concluded in

Adolph Sutro's great park on the hill, once meticulously landscaped, is now grown wild with fragrant eucalyptus (and dominated by the lanky television tower at its peak). The Sutro Baths, protected by glass from the Pacific winds, ingeniously engineered and heated, were a delight for generations of San Franciscans. They burned in 1966, after some years of declining popularity. Both the Cliff House and the melancholy ruins of the Sutro Baths are part of the Golden Gate National Recreation Area, a wonderful urban-centered park that comprises San Francisco's Ocean Beach, Sutro's old property, Angel and Alcatraz Islands, and the Marin Headlands.

short order. By withholding their labor, the unions had made a point even the most fustian employer could understand. Though they had not established a workers' paradise in San Francisco, the unions had achieved official recognition and political power. Following the strikes of 1901, San Francisco became, and has remained, one of the country's most unionized cities.

James Phelan had been unable to mediate the dispute. His failure cost him the crucial support of the business community in the 1901 elections. It is doubtful whether Phelen could have been reelected in any case, as the unions, united for the first time and eager to consolidate their gains, formed the Union Labor party to contest the first election of the century.

The Second Boss: Union Labor's ticket was headed by handsome Eugene Schmitz, conductor at the Columbia Theater and president of the Musician's Union. Except for his vast ignorance of practical politics, Schmitz was a perfect candidate. For one thing he was Irish-German, a fortuitous blending of the city's two major ethnic groups. For another, he was easily manipulated. Handy on the scene to do the manipulating was a lawyer named Abe Ruef, who had ingratiated himself with the Union Labor party since its inception.

Abe Ruef, San Francisco's second political boss, was a native San Franciscan, a graduate of the city's Hastings School of Law and, from the early age of twenty-two, a member of the bar. Like many, he seems to have graduated almost directly from idealism to cynicism; his senior thesis at the University of California had been "Purity in Politics." In the Union Labor party and its finely figured head, "Handsome Gene" Schmitz, Ruef saw the opportunity to test some of his newer theories of government. Speaking of Schmitz, Ruef once said, "The psychology of the mass of voters is like that of a crowd of small boys or primitive men. Other things being equal, of two candidates they will almost inevitably follow the fine, strongly built man."

Schmitz and his Union Labor ticket were elected in 1901, and by the time they were reelected in 1903, Ruef had firmly established himself as the power behind the throne. Ruef's power was based on his assiduous parcelling out of city contracts in return for kickbacks, and on his control over patronage. But he lacked the well-disciplined political machine that most eastern bosses enjoyed. The city's new supervisors were workingmen, unused to the temptations of power. And tempted they were. Before long they became known as the "Paint Eaters" from Ruef's plaintive comment that they were so greedy they would eat the paint off a house. Abe Ruef, a hard worker and a man with a decided talent for corruption, became ringmaster of a circus of greed. Four years into Union Labor's rule, the mad scramble for money had become a public spectacle. In 1905 the *Chronicle* zeroed in on Ruef:

> For four years it has been known that if one wanted anything which the administration was not compelled to grant, he must see Ruef. If you wish for a job for yourself or your friend, you must see Ruef. If you wish for a license for a grog-shop or a theater, you must see Ruef. If you desire to construct a building in defiance of the fire ordinances, you must see Ruef... His baleful influence covers our city like a pall.

The old reform group, now headed by James Phelan, Fremont Older, the crusading editor of the *Bulletin*, and Rudolph Spreckels, another new aristocrat, joined the *Chronicle*'s cry for reform.

In 1905 Schmitz and his ticket were reelected, to the dismay of the papers and the reformers. But Abe Ruef was having increasing difficulty keeping his Paint Eaters in a semblance of order. The structure of corruption seemed ready to collapse of its own weight. By early 1906, the reformers thought they were close to ending Boss Ruef's rule.

But civic reform had to be postponed while San Francisco coped with an unforeseen calamity. At 5:12 A.M. on April 18, while the footmen were still clearing the dinner plates from James Ben Ali Haggin's stable dinner party, as the denizens of the Barbary Coast were finishing their lecherous revels, while thousands of soberer citizens lay abed, the ancient fissure of the San Andreas fault slipped and the destruction of San Francisco began.

Ringmaster in a circus of greed: Boss Abe Ruef, looking less than trustworthy.

The Earthquake and Fire

6

San Francisco had long been acquainted with earthquakes. The Smithsonian Institution claimed that the city had experienced 465 temblors—most of them minor—since 1850. About that time, the *Annals of San Francisco* had warned of a coming disaster, but said that the "excitement-craving, money-seeking, luxurious-living, reckless heaven-earth-and-hell-daring citizens of San Francisco" were benumbed by the old maxim that "sufficient for the day is the evil thereof."

The jangly state of things made some people nervous. Robert Louis Stevenson contended that "earthquakes are common; the fear of them grows yearly in a resident; he begins with indifference and ends in sheer panic." But the city's last major quake had been in 1868 and most citizens were surely enjoying an unpanicked sleep when the first jolt hit at 5:12:06 on the morning of April 18, 1906.

For almost a minute the earth shook in the dreadfully total way of earthquakes. The San Andreas, the largest fault in a state streaked with faults, had slipped from Fort Bragg in the north to San Juan Bautista in the south, creating fright and havoc in an area 210 miles long and 30 miles wide.

Luckily, San Francisco doesn't lie directly on the San Andreas, but a little northeast of where it dives into the sea. Other towns in the area—San Jose to the south, little Point Reyes Station up north—suffered more from the quake than San Francisco. In fact, when the last brick had tumbled down, the city seemed to have come out fairly well. Its wooden houses had swayed and creaked, but most had remained standing.

The greatest damage occurred in North Beach and the financial district, where swampy marshes and the old Yerba Buena Cove had been filled in during the Gold Rush. The land there acted like jelly, trembling hideously,

Opposite page
The growing firestorm: Bystanders looked down earthquake-littered O'Farrell Street at the fire that within a few hours would all but level the heart of the city. (The tall building in the background is now called the Central Tower and houses this book's publishers.)

and magnifying the effects of the quake. Brick buildings collapsed, trolley tracks zig-zagged, and countless bottles in countless stores crashed to the floor. All over town windows shattered and china dishes fell to the ground. And the new City Hall—$8 million and twenty-nine years abuilding—gave up without a fight. It was later found that crates, newspapers, and other such materials had been liberally used in the great boondoggle. Not surprisingly, it was a total loss within seconds.

One of the few people killed by the quake itself was the city's fire chief, Dennis T. Sullivan, who had foreseen the calamitous aftermath of a major earthquake. Sullivan was mortally injured when a firehouse collapsed over his head, and the city's fire-bell system—as the chief had feared—was quickly put out of action.

When the terrifying rattling and rolling had stopped, many of the city's rudely awakened inhabitants began to assess the damage and perhaps hunt up a little breakfast. Photographer Arnold Genthe ambled over to the St. Francis, where free breakfast was being served by the hotel's unruffled waiters. In the lobby, he saw Enrico Caruso pacing about puffing a cigar. The night before, the great Italian tenor had performed Don Jose to Olive Fremsted's Carmen. On the fateful morning of the eighteenth, Genthe wrote, "It appeared that when he was awakened by the shock, [Caruso] had tried his vocal cords without success. ''Ell of a place! I never come back here.' And he never did."

Young John Barrymore, playing in *The Dictator*, was happily entertaining a few bottles of champagne and a young lady in his St. Francis hotel room when the quake struck. He used the ensuing chaos as a good excuse to hide out at a friend's house and go on one of his epic binges.

With the main quake finished (though the city weathered 120 aftershocks that day), San Francisco had reason to believe that it had gotten off lightly. But as dawn approached another disaster was gathering force. Had the earthquake been all—even with the panic and the lives lost in collapsed buildings—the city would soon have righted itself with typical "heaven-earth-and-hell-daring." But the earthquake itself accounted for only about 20 percent of the ruin San Francisco was about to suffer.

The marginal notes:

The 1906 earthquake has been estimated at 8.3 on the Richter Scale, a measurement devised years later. An earthquake of such magnitude today—and it is only a matter of time until one strikes—will be much more disastrous, given today's skyscrapers and increased population.

Actor John Barrymore later wrote a dramatic account of his adventures during the 1906 cataclysm, an account which he subsequently admitted was a product more of the bottle than of his actual experience.

The City Ablaze: As the city shook off the dust, as neighbors swapped stories and the unlucky picked through the rubble, the true calamity was showing itself: clouds of smoke began billowing up from the center of the city.

The breakfasts being cooked, the gas mains twisted and broken, the

Looking down Sacramento Street: In this famous picture Arnold Genthe caught the stunned disbelief of San Franciscans as they watched their city being destroyed.

hundreds of gas lanterns and candles fallen to the floor, had set fires all over San Francisco. In the heavily populated northeast quadrant, the heart of the city, fifty separate fires were soon burning out of control: the water mains that ran up to the city from the lower Peninsula thirty miles south were broken. There was no water pressure to fight the growing conflagration. The fire department, its chief dying, its warning system shattered, was helpless.

Soon the fires melted into two major blazes burning north, west, and south, threatening to devour the city. By afternoon, the financial district was a jungle of flame. The Palace Hotel, equipped with its own water supply, was bravely defended. But, when its wells ran dry, the Palace had to be abandoned. In North Beach, 36-year-old A. P. Giannini loaded the resources of his fledgling Bank of Italy into a cart to escape the fire.

By evening, the blazes had created a huge fire-storm. What didn't burn simply melted in the superheated air. The fire-storm spawned a horrifying sucking wind. Those wooden houses—90 percent of the city's homes—that had weathered the quake so well were pure kindling for the fire.

After 1906 more than 150 buried water cisterns, which appear as odd rings of brick from street level, were constructed at intersections all over San Francisco to insure a water supply when the next big earthquake occurs.

A.P. Giannini started his Bank of Italy—later, as the Bank of America, the biggest bank in the world—on its fabulous way by quickly investing $80,000 in rebuilding San Francisco.

Earthquake and Fire

Even as it had destroyed three-quarters of the city's residences, hotels, and lodging houses and most of its major businesses, the fire swept on. Fears grew that the fire would leap across the broad residential thoroughfare of Van Ness Avenue and burn—who knew?—perhaps to the ocean itself.

Mayor Schmitz, his political troubles for the moment in eclipse, responded well and calmly in the emergency. The mayor enlisted the help of General Frederick Funston's Presidio Army contingent to help patrol and prevent looting. On the afternoon of the eighteenth, Schmitz convened a meeting of the city's notables to plan relief measures. Schmitz diplomatically appointed his nemesis, urbane James Phelan, to head a "Citizens' Committee of Fifty," as it was called. The group hastily adjourned twice that day because of approaching flames. It finally ended up at the Fairmont Hotel—which itself was gutted by flames that very night.

The problems facing the committee were immense: where to house the streaming refugees, what to feed them, how to stop the fire. The committee first approved a proclamation by the mayor authorizing the Army, and the regular and special police to "KILL any and all persons found engaged in Looting or in the Commission of Any Other Crime." Gas and electric lines were to be shut off, a strict curfew imposed, and the populace warned of the danger of fire from damaged chimneys "or any like cause."

The Army hit upon the idea of trying to stop the fire's progress by dynamiting houses on the west side of Van Ness Avenue between Jackson and O'Farrell Streets. Their efforts were clumsy and crude—some say they actually encouraged the blaze—and appeared to be a failure. Then came a natural deliverance. The wind shifted and began to drive the fire back on itself. The western part of the city had been spared.

But for three days and two nights, the fire ate away at the northeast quadrant. In the end, the destruction was almost total. Almost: the antique buildings of Jackson Square escaped, as did the crests of Russian and Telegraph Hills, which were saved by independent water supplies and fortuitous winds. Some downtown structures, like the Call Building (now the Central Tower on Market Street) were gutted by fire but were later refurbished.

The Old Mint at Fifth and Mission (still standing today after 106 years) was spared, as was the United States Appraiser's Office at Washington and Sansome, defended valiantly by the Appraiser General John T. Dare and a crew of men using water from the building's roof tank, an island of sweating, cursing, scared men in a sea of fire.

The city's streets were clogged with dazed, unnaturally cheerful refugees. Years later Edward A. Hart, then nine and a half, remembered the scene: "Walking—away from the flames into the unaffected areas—we saw

"This man Schmitz had turned out pure gold in the emergency," Secretary of Commerce and Labor Victor Metcalf said later of San Francisco's crooked mayor.

In a nice San Francisco touch, threatened buildings on Telegraph Hill were draped with wine-soaked burlap to protect them from the fire.

A Short History of San Francisco

people in their houses, cleaning or reading . . . others in their front yards, talking, gossiping, wondering, but not concerned. It couldn't happen to them. But it did, and sooner than anyone would anticipate."

As the fire approached, people grabbed what they could, what in the confused moment seemed dearest: caged birds and heirloom china, framed pictures and children's toys. In Chinatown, women with bound feet, incapable of walking, were being manhandled through the streets to safety.

Thousands fled the city in the ferry boats leaving from blessedly intact wharves. From the shores of Marin and Oakland, they looked back in fascinated horror at the towering clouds and squirming flames destroying their city; it was a tragic but, many remembered, a perversely beautiful sight.

A. Area burned by fire
B. Van Ness Avenue

The Phoenix Rises Again: An estimated 250,000 San Franciscans (out of a total population of less than 400,000) were left homeless by the three days of destruction. Army and civil authorities erected tent cities in San Francisco's parks to shelter the stricken but well-behaved refugees. Seventy thousand people camped in the Presidio alone, tens of thousands in Portsmouth Square, Mission Park, Golden Gate Park, and the homes and gardens of fortunate friends.

Thanks in large part to Mayor Schmitz and the dedication of the Committee of Fifty, the relief of San Francisco was a huge, complex, and by all accounts orderly affair. Food was scarce, but there was no widespread hunger. Relief kitchens (sporting such names as "The New Poodle Dog," and "Delmonico's") were set up all over town. The nation and the world responded charitably to San Francisco's plight. As news of the catastrophe reached them, San Francisco's eastern neighbors began collecting food and clothing and loading it onto westbound trains. Over $100 million, plus untold amounts of supplies, were donated from the States (including $31,000 from the country's schoolchildren toward the reconstruction of the city's schools). Fourteen other nations sent over half a million dollars.

San Franciscans faced the catastrophe with typical verve and pluck. Lawrence W. Harris wrote a poem which praised "the damndest finest ruins ever gazed on anywhere," and maintained "I would rather bore a hole/And live right in the ashes than ever more to Oakland's mole." Even in the midst of tragedy and dislocation, San Francisco didn't forget to look down upon its transbay neighbor. Another sign read, "Eat, Drink and Be Merry For Tomorrow We May Have to Go to Oakland."

For six weeks, no indoor fires were allowed anywhere in the city for fear of new fires caused by faulty gas lines and broken chimneys. San Francisco

Rebuilding on Post Street:
The ashes were still warm
when San Francisco began
reconstructing itself.

Rebuilding on Post Street: The ashes were still warm when San Francisco began reconstructing itself.

enjoyed a brief return to Gold Rush democracy as all classes and races mixed and chatted at the sidewalk kitchens. Edward Hart remembered the adventure of it all and recalled the melancholy when "the stoves could be brought back into the house from the sidewalk . . . when that day came . . . that was THE day . . . the streets looked empty."

When the fires finally burned themselves out, when all or almost all had been accounted for, the city took stock. Almost 500 people had died. An area of over 500 square blocks, the kernel of the city, had burned, destroying more than 28,000 buildings. Estimates of the financial loss ranged from $350 to $500 million. Four-fifths of San Francisco's property had gone up in smoke.

A Short History of San Francisco

But San Francisco, burned six times in the 1850s, was after all the city with a "Phoenix issuing from flames" on its city seal. No one doubted that the city would rise again, and little time was lost getting at it. Arnold Genthe wrote that "rebuilding started while the ruins were still smoking. On top of a heap of collapsed walls, a sign would announce, 'On this site will be erected a six-story office building to be ready for occupancy in the Fall.'"

Clean-up crews worked around the clock clearing the smoldering debris from downtown and dumping it in the Bay. Temporary tracks were laid on broken streets. A building boom was in the offing. In early 1906, the city had 20,000 construction workers. At the end of the year, there were 60,000. Wages returned to the inflated levels they had reached during the madness of the Gold Rush, as rebuilding continued feverishly.

Although Mayor Schmitz (a teetotaler) had ordered the city's saloons to close for three months, the old "intensified pursuit of human happiness" went on: 220 marriage licenses were issued in the first ten postquake days; on April 24th, the Chutes gave its first vaudeville performance. The chic downtown stores—Gump's, W. & J. Sloane, City of Paris, Shreve—quickly set up shop in the fancy mansions on the west side of Van Ness. Business was business after all, and novelist Charles Dobie reported that the fire hadn't much changed San Franciscan tastes. The merchants, he wrote, were pleased to find that "silk gowns sold, but wash dresses languished on their shelves."

The city's determination to get on with business and pleasure as usual was astounding. Within three years of the Fire, $150 million worth of new buildings had been constructed, many of the Class A (fire-resistant steel or reinforced concrete). Nineteen thousand new wood frame buildings had been built, and fewer than eight thousand of the 28,000 destroyed buildings remained to be replaced.

As in the past, the debris of the 1906 disaster became landfill and was built upon. The buildings erected on that fill are especially vulnerable to a new quake.

The City Beautiful: But the rush to rebuild, admirable in its pluck and energy, meant that a marvelous opportunity was missed—a chance to rebuild the city with an eye to beauty. In the haste to get business cranked up again, San Francisco was following those same old unimaginative grid patterns so beloved of speculators, so unsuited to the city's graceful figure.

Since well before the fire, the "City Beautiful" movement, led by James Phelan and others of refined temperament, had been lobbying for at least a partial rejection of the grids and a coordinated effort to redeem the glorious natural promise which had been lost in the mindless explosion of San Francisco.

Earthquake and Fire

The City Beautiful:
Daniel Burnham's plan for
Telegraph Hill is a delightful exercise in grand, un-
tethered thinking.

A Short History of San Francisco

The flower of the City Beautiful movement was the Burnham Plan, the creation of renowned city planner Daniel H. Burnham. In 1904 Phelan had invited Burnham from Chicago to create a master plan for San Francisco. He was installed in a cottage high on Twin Peaks, where he had a matchless panorama of the upper Peninsula. For almost two years Burnham cogitated and sketched and discussed his vision with a group of the city's vital new generation of architects, men like Bernard Maybeck and the eccentric genius Willis Polk.

Burnham's dictum was "Make no little plans" and his vision of San Francisco's future, unveiled in book form in 1905, fit that philosophy. The Burnham Plan envisioned hilltops free of development, grandly heroic boulevards leading from a neoclassical City Center, towers and colonnades and, of course, many new streets that gently followed the contours of the land, rather than barging up and down.

It would have been wildly expensive, true, but the Burnham Plan was a fascinating possibility and had wide support. Old Hubert Howe Bancroft, never one given to pipe dreams, gave it his characteristically pecuniary approval: "Let us have the City Beautiful by all means—it will pay."

But the fire instead doomed the Burnham Plan. The smoke had hardly cleared when it became obvious that the city wouldn't sit still, couldn't wait to rebuild. Burnham's dazzling vision was washed away in the tide of business as usual.

So, with barely a condescending nod in the direction of the City Beautiful, San Francisco kept true to its somehow heartening lack of foresight—its birthmark as an instant city. It rebuilt, new and better, but much the same as before. Even the frenetic desire to get on with it could never destroy the city's beauty. And—most important—the old bird rose and flew yet again.

Willis Polk among other achievements remodeled the Flood mansion and in 1918 built one of San Francisco's architectural landmarks, the Hallidie Building at 130 Sutter Street, one of the first "hanging glass" buildings, and still a fascinating mixture of inspired modernity and late Victorian decoration.

The Second Century

7

As impatient as it was to get on with rebuilding itself following the fire, San Francisco had some unfinished business to attend to. Boss Ruef, "Handsome Gene" Schmitz, and their flock of Paint Eaters were still in office. They weren't going to be spared the clean-up fever.

Shortly before the fire, the city's reformers had enlisted Francis J. Heney, a prominent federal prosecutor, to lead a legal assault against corruption. Heney hired the great detective William Burns (who later founded the Burns Detective Agency) and installed a new grand jury. In November, seven months after the fire, Ruef and Schmitz were indicted on a series of bribery and graft charges.

In June 1907, after a wonderfully spicy trial, Mayor Schmitz was convicted of taking kickbacks from some of the city's French restaurants—eateries that featured upstairs entertainment of a nonculinary sort. Schmitz had made sure they got liquor licenses (what was a French restaurant without French champagne? it was asked) and in return they allegedly showed their appreciation in a number of ways, of which pure money was not the least (Schmitz was, after all, a teetotaler).

But it appears that in his rush to escort Schmitz to the cooler, Heney had trampled on the law. At least the Court of Appeals and later all seven members of the California Supreme Court thought so. Schmitz's conviction was overturned in early 1908.

Boss Ruef wasn't so lucky. Before the fire, Ruef had convinced the Board of Supervisors to allow the United Railroads Company to switch from underground cables to overhead electric lines. For his well-oiled persuasiveness, Ruef was awarded $200,000, some of which later found its way into the supervisors' pockets.

Opposite page
Spanning the Golden Gate: During the greatest depression in history, San Francisco and her neighbors built two of the greatest bridges in history, the Golden Gate and Bay bridges.

It has never made good political sense to meddle with San Francisco's cable cars, and when Ruef arrogantly had United Railroads' authorization renewed after the fire, he was yanked into court and convicted of bribery in December 1908. Ruef played out his full skein of appeals, but in mid-1911 the doors of San Quentin prison shut behind him. A "model prisoner," Ruef served four and a half years.

The Graft Trials had begun with a righteous fanfare and a storm of indictments—3,000 were eventually issued. For a time they were high civic drama, especially when Francis Heney was shot in the head by an ex-convict who had been dismissed as a juror. The already murky atmosphere surrounding the trials was darkened when Heney's assailant committed suicide and the city's police chief mysteriously died.

But as time passed, as the Ruef and Schmitz trials ended and the minutiae—what table in what restaurant, what kind of envelope—took over, the trials became a bore. And, since graft works two ways, some very powerful men found themselves under scrutiny. That meant high-priced lawyers and delays, and, perhaps coincidently, the mysterious disappearance of witnesses and evidence, not to mention a distressing number of bombings, threats, and attempted bribes. The Graft Trials—by damn—were becoming "bad for business." By 1909 they were as good as over.

Of the whole crew, only Abe Ruef ever did time in prison. Fremont Older of the *Bulletin*, ever the foe of corruption and inequity, saw the injustice of this and agitated successfully for Ruef's parole. Following his release in 1915, the old boss rented an office in the Columbus Tower at Kearny and Columbus and became a purveyor of "ideas" and real estate. His once substantial fortune dwindled over the years (with some help from the Depression) and he died impoverished in 1936.

Eugene Schmitz's reputation is undergoing a mild revival these days, the thinking being that he was rather too slow a mind to have been much of a crook. In any case, he must have had his defenders even then, as he was elected to the Board of Supervisors in 1917 and served eight years. He died in 1928 of a heart condition.

The Era of "Sunny Jim": The Graft Trials were a nagging hangover from prefire days. With a new city built (bigger and better!) and the corruptionists out of the way, the city could turn to more edifying pursuits. A fresh dose of prosperity was on its way: the War To End War (the first) was going to provide a gory stimulus to the Port of San Francisco, and the dizzy affluence of the 1920s would inflate San Francisco along with the rest of the country. In the mayoral elections of 1911, the city elected a perfect complement to the jolly coming prosperity.

James Rolph, called "Sunny Jim" for his ceaseless good fellowship, was to serve five terms as mayor. He had been a mildly successful businesman who had made a reputation organizing relief after the fire. Following the urging of his friends, Sunny Jim then dropped his oar in political waters.

For times that weren't too demanding of a city father, James Rolph was a natural. While not burdened with an excess of brains, he kept the city in one piece and provided the government-with-a-sly-wink that San Francisco wanted during the 1920s. He could be counted on to cut ribbons with a flourish, deliver a nicely florid speech, slap backs, and make sure the coarser elements kept in their place. He was a great supporter of the virtues of the time: progress, size, and the right of the businessman to operate as he saw fit.

Perennial mayor: "Sunny Jim" Rolph (left, with his chief of police, "Uncle Danny" O'Brien), looking typically outlandish in the infield.

Sunny Jim was a natty, if somewhat eccentric, dresser. He always wore a fresh flower in his lapel, draped his extensive frame with expensive suits and sported brightly polished cowboy boots whatever the occasion. He wanted—everyone seemed to want—a town that was neither too open nor too shut. This was the era of prohibition, to which San Francisco took like a cat to water. It certainly wasn't going to be Sunny Jim's boys who shut the town up tight. As Sally Stanford, a famous San Francisco madam and a great friend of the perennial mayor, wrote in her autobiography *The Lady of the House*, Rolph's "attitudes were the most significant thing about him. First and foremost, he was for Live and Let Live, Let Sleeping Dogs Lie, and Don't Stir Up Muddy Waters. Also, If You Haven't Tried It Don't Knock It." Not an exalted philosophy perhaps, but one well suited to the intensified pursuit of certain kinds of human happiness.

With an accommodating, expansive mayor like Sunny Jim at the helm, San Francisco was ready to get on with its great building projects of the next decades. What better way to celebrate San Francisco's rebirth than with the construction of a new and glorious city hall? The capitalists and bankers and builders were in agreement with the aesthetes of the City Beautiful movement here. San Francisco needed something dignified and grand, as befitted the metropolis of the west, not another shoddy gimcrack like the old city hall. In 1912 the city's voters approved an $8 million bond issue to finance a whole civic complex, to be located on the site of the old city hall ruin. The architectural firm of Bakewell and Brown was chosen from among many competitors to design the new city hall. Both Arthur Brown and John Bakewell had been educated in Europe and their design drew heavily on Old World motifs. They also—and this was important in those days—kept within their $3.5 million budget.

San Francisco's new city hall was dedicated on December 29, 1915. It was hailed from the beginning as a masterpiece. Substantial yet graceful, the French Renaissance (or, depending on the authority, classical baroque) structure, with its forthright ornamentation and majestic central staircase, is one of America's most beautiful and imposing municipal buildings.

City Hall was the center piece of the ambitious Civic Center complex. The Exposition Auditorium (now called the Civic Auditorium) had preceded it by a year. Then followed the main branch of the Public Library (notable for its prodigal use of space), the California State Building, the Veterans' Memorial Building (home of the San Francisco Museum of Modern Art) and, finally, in 1932, the Opera House, where, in June 1945, fifty-one nations (guided by Temporary Secretary-general Alger Hiss) signed the Charter of the United Nations, an event commemorated by the new United Nations Plaza just off Market Street.

The Panama-Pacific International Exposition: San Francisco has never been a city to wallow in false modesty. From the beginning, it willingly conducted the chorus of its praises: it had its Sam Brannans, boosting and bragging, its Billy Ralstons trying to make it into a westernized Paris and its M. H. de Youngs wanting, of all things, to celebrate its winter climate. Even before the fire, San Francisco had been in the mood for a giant celebration of its own good luck at being itself—and, incidentally, the completion of the Panama Canal.

In 1904 the city had petitioned Congress to designate San Francisco the official site of a world's fair to mark the canal's opening. The fair enthusiasts were looking ahead: the Panama Canal wasn't scheduled to be completed for another eleven years.

The fire interrupted those plans, but not for long: on the fourth anniversary of the great catastrophe, April 18, 1910, $4 million of Panama-Pacific International Exposition stock was eagerly snapped up by San Franciscans. The city's pluck impressed the state legislature, which weighed in with favorable legislation. In early January 1911, Congress named San Francisco the official site of a world's fair to celebrate the canal and—though it wouldn't do to brag about it—San Francisco's incredible renaissance.

All San Francisco's postfire phoenix energy and all of Sunny Jim's thundering good will were set to the task of hosting and impressing the world. President Taft sent out an invitation to the family of nations to participate. The Exposition Company, flush and confident, bought up over 600

acres of ancient tidal land called Harbor Cove, stretching along the northern waterfront from Fort Mason to the Golden Gate. A stone retaining wall was built and the marshy land topped with soil . . . suddenly there was a perfect site for a fair.

A distinguished panel of architects was chosen to supervise and harmonize building. One of its inspired choices was Paris-educated Bernard Maybeck, one of California's most inventive architects. Maybeck was commissioned to design the exposition's centerpiece, the Palace of Fine Arts. He responded with a magnificent neoclassical rotunda and elegant colonnades set by a lagoon. The business part of the Palace—where the art exhibits were displayed—was an undistinguished shedlike building behind the gloriously

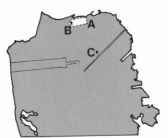

A. Panama-Pacific
   International
   Exposition
B. Palace of Fine Arts
C. Civic Center

When the Panama-Pacific International Exposition's fairy-tale lights were extinguished and its splendid buildings razed, the city sold the reclaimed marsh land on which it had been held for a tidy profit. The present-day Marina District is built on the site. The Palace of Fine Arts—meant to symbolize the "mortality of grandeur"—is the only major remnant of the exposition. Saved from the wreckers, it slowly and majestically decayed until the 1960s, when financier Walter Johnson donated $2.5 million toward its restoration. Today it is the home of the San Francisco International Film Festival, the Exploratorium, and a host of temporary exhibits and special events.

nonfunctional rotunda. Maybeck's haunting building symbolized, as he intended it to, the "mortality of grandeur and the vanity of human wishes."

The Palace of Fine Arts was the artistic heart of the exposition, but the 432-foot Tower of Jewels dominated it physically. Encrusted with 50,000 pieces of colored glass, washed at night by the prepsychedelic lights of thirty-six tinted spotlights, it was designed to, and did, inspire rapture and astonishment. And there were the exposition's other major buildings, the Palaces of Industry and Horticulture and Education, all done in imitation marble, indirectly lit (a great novelty for the time), part of a harmonious dream-city. It was a marvelous place to stroll, taking in the ornamental charm of the buildings and the delicious landscaping, a product of Uncle John McLaren, who planted 30,000 trees on the old swamp and imported an ark of exotic flora from around the world, including 70,000 rhododendrons from Holland.

The Panama-Pacific International Exposition, to many the most wonderful world's fair in history, opened on February 20, 1915. Despite fears that the war in Europe would force some of the twenty-five participating nations to withdraw, only a few did, and the exposition was a grand success. On opening day, nearly a quarter of a million people visited the wonderland on the shores of San Francisco Bay. Poet Edwin Markham was moved to write:

I have seen tonight the greatest revelation of beauty that has ever been seen on the earth. I may say this literally and with full regard for all that is known of ancient art and architecture and all that the modern world has heretofore seen of glory and grandeur. I have seen beauty that will give the world new standards of art and a joy in loveliness never before reached. That is what I have seen.

Markham was known for his unchained enthusiasms, but he wasn't alone in being overwhelmed by the exposition. Today, photographs and memoirs evoke an enchanting place, a mixture of delicacy and magnificence, of pure fun and high purpose, of a kind of exuberant taste rarely found in such an event. And there is always the Palace of Fine Arts, quietly nostalgic for some never-never time, causing, as its creater intended, a certain "sadness modified by the feeling that beauty has a soothing influence."

The exposition ran for nine months and twelve days. True, it had celebrated the Panama Canal (with a five-acre working model) but, more important, it had announced to the world that one of its favorite cities, the City of Gold, the fabled Instant City, had risen from the ashes and rebuilt itself in high style.

A Short History of San Francisco

Mooney and Billings: The exposition was amazing in many ways, perhaps—to modern sensibilities at least—most of all because it actually turned a profit. But those were the days of boosterism and babbittry, when profitmaking was a holy consummation, the very cornerstone in the American edifice. As Sunny Jim said at one of his ribbon-cuttings, "Prosperity for the businessman... means prosperity for all."

But the mayor's chirpy creed had its share of heretics. The city's unions, in eclipse since the disgrace of the Union Labor party, were stirring once again. In June 1916 a series of strikes led to the formation of a Law and Order Committee made up of well-heeled businessmen dedicated to the "open shop" (which meant the freedom to hire strike-breakers). The committee raised $1.5 million to combat the strikes and didn't hesitate to wave the red flag: even picketing was "an act of violence."

Tension finally exploded into violence on July 22, 1916. The occasion, a parade marking Preparedness Day, at first seems an odd flash point between business and labor. But many unionists opposed the Preparedness Day craze then prevalent in America. They feared that preoccupation with war was an excuse to squelch unionism in the name of patriotism. When San Francisco's parade was announced, one union man summed up the opposition: "Our protests have been in regard to Preparedness Day propaganda, so we are going to use a little direct action on the 22nd to show that militarism can't be forced on us and our children without violent protest."

The protest, if that's what it was meant to be, was indeed direct and violent. At 2 P.M., as Governor Hiram Johnson and a beaming, strutting Jim Rolph led a mile-long parade down Market Street near the Ferry Building, a pipe bomb exploded. Ten people were killed and more than forty injured.

Amidst all the civic and national clamor, it was generally conceded that unionists were surely behind the dastardly crime. So two logical candidates for guilt were quickly located, arrested, tried, and convicted. Tom Mooney and Warren Billings were likely suspects; both had been tried for sabotage, and Billings had just been let out of Folsom prison, where he had been serving a sentence for bombing.

Mooney, sentenced to be executed, and Billings, who got life imprisonment, became the Sacco and Vanzetti of the west, and to people all over the world their imprisonment symbolized a convergence of evils: capitalism, militarism, wild west justice, and militant antiunionism. Governor William Stephens reduced Mooney's sentence to life imprisonment in 1918 at the urging of President Wilson, who said the case had "assumed international proportions." But the wheels of injustice ground on. In 1928 Mooney's trial judge, Franklin Griffen, wrote that "every witness who testified against

Mooney has been shown to have testified falsely. There is no evidence against him. There is no serious suggestion that any exists."

For over two decades, "Free Tom Mooney" was a labor rallying cry. But Tom Mooney in San Quentin and Warren Billings in Folsom moldered away. The mere question of their innocence or guilt was often lost in politics, ideology, and a widespread distaste for such quarrelsome malcontents as Billings and Mooney were popularly supposed to be.

Finally, in January 1939, Governor Culbert Olson fulfilled a campaign pledge by pardoning Mooney and reducing Billing's sentence to time served. Mooney, nearly sixty years old, enfeebled by prison and often irritatingly cranky, proved a better symbol than leader. He died three years after leaving prison. Billings quietly turned to watch-repairing, and died in 1972, a reminder to the end of a shameful episode in American justice.

Imprisoned radical Mooney, in particular, wasn't always his own best advocate. San Francisco sheriff Daniel Murphy is supposed to have said, "For years I have had one great ambition. Now I have two. The first is to free Tom Mooney. The second is to kick his ass in the Bay."

The ILA and Bloody Thursday: The Preparedness Day bombing was a setback for labor. So, too, in a more subtle way, was World War I, which, like the Spanish-American War, brought prosperity to the Port of San Francisco. In the decade of 1910–20, San Francisco's population rose by 20 percent. Following the war, San Francisco shared in the frantic prosperity of the 1920s. The city was used to the giddy highs of good fortune and the frenzy of a stock exchange drunk on ever-rising values, and it joined right in on the national frolic of the Roaring Twenties.

Sunny Jim oversaw it all like a harmlessly lecherous uncle, keeping everybody happy, dashing around town in his official limousine (more often than not in the company of some pliant young lass), checking his favorite hangouts, bombastic, bountiful, and, in the way he fit the times, beautiful.

But those innocent times changed with sickening rapidity. In 1929 the stock market crash pushed America into the Great Depression. Economic disaster crept into San Francisco like a deadly, confident fog. Shipping was down. Montgomery Street, the Wall Street of the west, was struck dumb. Thousands were laid off, in San Francisco, in California, all across the nation.

Sunny Jim Rolph, though he didn't know it, was already a relic of happier days. In 1931 he was elected governor of California. His native incompetence, little noticed during flush times, bloomed in Sacramento. Hale fellowship and blustery confidence were no defense against a depression; Rolph fought with the unions, he fought with the legislature, and gradually faded like a hot house bloom in the cold reality of hard times. In 1933 Rolph used up most of what remained of his political stock by stupidly defending the lynching of two murder suspects in San Jose. "This is the best lesson that California has ever given the country," said the old, suddenly less entertaining blowhard. In 1934 he died of a heart attack, and with him passed an era.

Nowhere was the tragedy of the Depression more apparent than on the waterfront, still the foundation of the city's economy. With the decline in shipping, 4,000 longshoremen were forced to compete for 1,300 jobs. The company-dominated Longshoremen's Association of San Francisco (the despised Blue Book Union, so called for the color of its dues book) played a cynical game of divide and conquer. Troublemakers were denied jobs; only the compliant got work on the "star gangs," and then often at the price of kickbacks to the union.

As the Depression wore on, a brilliant Australian-born organizer named Harry Bridges set to work resurrecting the moribund International Longshoreman's Association as a worker-controlled counter to the Blue Book Union. By 1934 the ILA and Harry Bridges had gained primacy on the waterfront. The time had come at last to force the issues.

In May the ILA struck the Pacific coast's ports. The union's demands were simple: six-hour days, 30-hour weeks, a $1 minimum wage with $1.50 overtime. Most crucial to the establishment of union power on the waterfront, however, were the ILA demands that the union control the hiring halls (and so end the star gangs) and that the ports become closed shops (ending the use of scab labor).

The strike was a success. As William Camp wrote in *San Francisco, Port of Gold*, "Longshoremen in Seattle, Bellingham, Tacoma, Aberdeen, Astoria, Gray's Harbor, San Francisco, San Pedro, Stockton, Oakland and San Diego arose as usual and went towards the waterfront. They gathered as usual at piers and waterfront sheds but they did not report for work. The strike was solid all up and down the coast."

Twelve thousand striking longshoremen, held fast by necessity and the organizing genius of Harry Bridges, were soon joined by sympathetic unions. In the strikes of 1901, the maritime unions had joined the striking Teamsters, and now, thirty-three years later, the Teamsters repaid the favor by refusing to haul to and from the docks.

The waterfront employers and the city's newspapers—led by the now bitterly antiunion *Examiner*—were apoplectic over the ILA's success. The strike had shut down San Francisco's most treasured asset: the port was losing $700,000 a day. In July the Industrial Association, last flower of the union-busting employers, decided to put a stop to the strike. It hired a gang of toughs, formed the Atlas Trucking Company (scab from top to bottom), and announced, somewhat prematurely, that "The Port of San Francisco is

On the waterfront: Longshoremen marched in protest along the Embarcadero just before Bloody Thursday.

now open to the business of San Francisco." On July 5, 1934, "Bloody Thursday," the Industrial Association attempted to ram its trucks through the picket lines at Pier 38. So began a brutal waterfront war.

Angry, club-wielding men, both union and scab, rampaged through the streets. Police on horseback added to the confusion of milling crowds, tear gas, fires, and overturned trucks. "Blood ran red in the streets of San Francisco," Royce Brier wrote the next day in the *Chronicle*. It was "the darkest day this city has known since April 18, 1906." More than 100 men were injured and two were killed in the fighting. But, in the end, despite the best efforts of the employers and their thugs, the picket lines held.

Eleven days after "Bloody Thursday," the ILA—still fighting the long war—boldly called a city-wide general strike. It, too, was successful. Theaters, liquor stores, groceries, and all but nineteen of the city's 200 restaurants closed. It was, and remains, the largest general strike in American history. For all its effectiveness, the strike soon became unpopular, and after

A Short History of San Francisco

four days it was called off. But Harry Bridges and the ILA had won their war. The long struggle on the waterfront was over. The employers agreed to almost all the union demands, including the critical issues of union-controlled hiring halls and the institution of the closed shop.

Union power had been reestablished in San Francisco and the ILA (today the International Longshoremen's and Warehousemen's Union) became one of the country's most powerful unions. But for decades Harry Bridges was a lightning rod for controversy and hate. He was hounded by threats of deportation on the grounds that he was a communist. Yet by the time he retired in 1977, Harry Bridges, still as cantankerous as ever, had become a respected and admired civic leader.

Buildings and Bridges: Despite its bouts with labor strife and Depression, San Francisco retained a phenomenal energy during the 1930s. It was, after all, nearly as used to hard as to good times, and (maybe it was that comforting old maxim "sufficient to the day is the evil thereof") the city never seemed to suffer quite as much as the rest of the country.

As always, it was a city of delights, old and new. What gloom there was might be dispelled by, say, going to see Joe DiMaggio and the other Seals play topflight baseball down at Seals Stadium at 16th and Bryant, sampling the bounteous restaurants of North Beach (50¢, including wine), swimming at the Sutro Baths or the Crystal Plunge (the home of Olympic champions), or dancing under the stars at Marin's romantic Rose Bowl. Despite the Depression, there was little hesitant or unsure about San Francisco in the 1930s. It was a time when the city not only enjoyed itself as usual, but bravely launched some of its most ambitious building projects.

One of that era's most charming artifacts is Coit Tower, built atop Telegraph Hill in 1933. No tourist would miss a visit to the tower: for the sublime view, for the WPA murals inside, and for the just slightly odd aura that surrounds it. Lillie Coit, for whom the tower is named, was an odd one herself. San Francisco's reigning madcap heiress during the 1860s and 1870s, she often dressed in male drag so she could infiltrate the town's racier nightspots. Another of her enthusiasms was chasing fire wagons. Her affection for San Francisco's valiant firemen was such that when the Knicker-bocker Number Five Fire Company made her an honorary member, she took to signing her name Lillie Hancock Coit Knickerbocker. She died in 1929, at the age of eighty-six, leaving a $100,000 bequest to build a tower in honor of her firefighting friends.

In recent years, the Port of San Francisco has had a rough time of it. The tourist industry centered around Fisherman's Wharf is doing well, as usual. But there hasn't been much fishing out of the wharf for years, and the business of the port has fallen on hard times. Its once unchallenged supremacy on the Pacific coast is over. The Port of Oakland, which switched to containerized shipping early on—something San Francisco has yet to do—surpassed San Francisco in gross tonnage in 1969, and has been increasing its lead ever since. Whether the cause of the port's decline is poor management, lack of space, or rapacious unions, the end of San Francisco as a major port city is a sad thing.

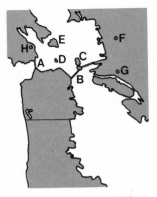

A. Golden Gate Bridge
B. Bay Bridge
C. Treasure Island
D. Alcatraz Island
E. Angel Island
F. Oakland
G. Berkeley
H. Sausalito

Just after Coit Tower was finished, a far less delightful building project began on Alcatraz Island, once the peaceful home of the Bay's pelicans. In 1934 the federal government took over the island from the Army (which had been using it as a military prison since 1886) and began building cells to house its worst felons. For three decades the escape-proof island—tantalizingly within sight of the city's dazzling lights—was the home of 370 or so criminals, among them Al Capone and the legendary "Birdman of Alcatraz," Robert Stroud.

In 1963 the inefficient and decaying prison was abandoned (to the relief of those who prefer to see the Bay graced by something besides a penitentiary). The island was occupied by militant American Indians from 1969–71, then became a popular tourist attraction while the federal government was trying to decide what to do with it—as it still is.

The same year Alcatraz was being turned into America's Devil's Island, the first clear Sierra water arrived in San Francisco, carried more than 150 miles from the mountains, across the Central Valley to the Peninsula and up to the city by the massive Hetch Hetchy water project, begun in 1914. The success of the Hetch Hetchy project solved San Francisco's nagging water supply problem (and gave it a valuable source of hydroelectric power), but it was nonetheless bitterly controversial. For the system's main reservoir is the flooded Hetch Hetchy Valley, near Yosemite Valley, generally considered second only to the Yosemite in splendor. John Muir was shocked by plans to turn the valley into a lake, "Dam the Hetch Hetchy!" he wrote, "As well dam for water tanks the people's cathedrals and churches, for no holier temple has ever been consecrated by the heart of man." After years of protest and litigation, the Hetch Hetchy was flooded during the 1920s. The long and angry conflict over the whole development project foreshadowed the conflict between development and conservation that was to explode later in the century.

But it was the construction of San Francisco's two great bridges, the San Francisco-Oakland Bay Bridge and the magnificent Golden Gate Bridge, that dominated the city's imagination and energy in the 1930s. The need for bridges to span the Bay had long been obvious. In the 1870s, Emperor Norton had decreed, "Now, therefore, we, Emperor Norton of the United States and Protector of Mexico, do order and direct . . . that a bridge be constructed from . . . Oakland Point to Yerba Buena [San Francisco], from thence to the mountain range of Sausalito, and from thence to the Farallones."

The old mental case's prophetic command took sixty years to obey. Until the 1930s, the technology needed to build bridges across the Bay simply didn't exist. As the region's population grew, the Bay's ferry boats

A Short History of San Francisco

handled a staggering amount of traffic. By the late 1920s, fifty million people a year were using the ferries, and the Ferry Building was the busiest transit station in the United States. But this was the age of the automobile, and the ferries couldn't hope to compete with the quickness and ease promised by transbay bridges.

In May of 1933, construction of the Bay Bridge was at last begun. First a relatively simple cantilever bridge was built from Oakland to Yerba Buena Island—a convenient anchorage about halfway between Oakland and San Francisco. A tunnel seventy-six feet high and fifty-eight feet wide, still the largest bore in the world, was dug through the island.

The most daunting task was the construction of a suspension bridge from Yerba Buena Island to Rincon Hill in San Francisco. First a massive concrete pier, 400 feet tall (half of it under water) was built to anchor the twin suspension spans. According to John Bernard McGloin, S.J., in his book *San Francisco, The Story of a City*, the pier is bulkier than the largest Egyptian pyramid, and more concrete was used in its construction than on the Empire State Building.

The pier's foundations had to be sunk deep into the mud, down to bedrock; when completed, they were the deepest foundations on earth. They had to be, for the Bay was the deepest body of water ever spanned. With the all-important pier in place, the building of the four 500-foot towers and the bridge's suspended double-tiered roadways could begin.

When the Bay Bridge was completed in November 1936, three years, four months, and three days after construction began, its eight and a half miles of steel, sweat, and inspiration had cost almost $80 million, up to that time, according to Father McGloin, "the greatest expenditure of funds ever used for the construction of a single structure in the history of man."

For all its majesty, the Bay Bridge is overshadowed by the lyrical and delicate Golden Gate Bridge. Of course, it has the advantage of a unique setting. When dreams of a bridge to span the Golden Gate began to get serious, many in fact opposed gilding one of nature's fairest lillies. Author Katherine Gerould, for one, wrote:

When you have one of the most romantic approaches in all geography, why spoil it? Let the landowners of lovely Marin stew in their own juice. Make the Sausalito ferry a "floating palace," beguile the half-hour journey with every vulgar pleasure; subsidize the communities if necessary; but in the interest of your own uniqueness, dear San Francisco, do not bridge the Golden Gate.

But the landowners of Marin and the four counties to the north—Napa,

Sonoma, Mendocino, and tiny Del Norte on the Oregon border—weren't content to stew in their own juices. The "Redwood Empire" insisted that Highway 101, which would link the state from north to south, shouldn't be broken at the Golden Gate. So, in 1928, the four northern counties joined with San Francisco to form the Golden Gate Bridge and Highway District. Two years later, the Bridge District voted a $35 million bond issue to finance the bridge. Joseph Baerman Strauss, a diminutive, world-famous bridge builder who had been planning and meditating on a Golden Gate Bridge since 1917, was chosen to oversee the vast project. Strauss was a poet; the Golden Gate demanded no less.

Construction of what for many years would be the world's longest suspension bridge began in early January 1933. Every aspect of the building was difficult: the great heights demanded courage and athletic prowess, the engineering had to be utterly meticulous, the foundations for the twin 746-foot towers (191 feet taller than the Washington Monument) had to be sunk in the midst of a narrow and turbulent strait, whose tides daily expel an amount of water seven times greater than does the Mississippi at its mouth. To protect his towers from the rushing waters, Strauss constructed two ingenious football-field-sized "fenders," a masterful and difficult solution to his major problem.

For almost four and a half years San Francisco and the world watched in awe as the graceful structure took shape. In February 1937 ten men were killed when a scaffolding gave way. But work continued. Enough steel wire to circle the earth three times was used to support the bridge's roadway, a dizzying 220 feet above the ocean. When the bridge was opened to exclusively pedestrian traffic (for the first and last time) on May 27, 1937, a quarter of a million Californians walked in gleeful admiration over that thin but strong roadway. They saw what was, and is, an extraordinary rarity: a work of man that enhances rather than detracts from the work of nature.

Treasure Island: In the midst of the worst depression in history, San Francisco and its sibling cities around the Bay had built the two greatest bridges on earth. Typically, San Francisco chose to celebrate its achievement with a giant party—another world's fair, in fact.

In 1934 an organizing committee chose Yerba Buena Shoals as the site for a fair. The shoals were 400-odd acres of murk and muck conveniently adjacent to Yerba Buena Island and the Bay Bridge. For three years, sand and silt was dredged from the Bay and pumped onto the shoals to create a man-made island, given the magical name Treasure Island.

The Golden Gate International Exposition (most people just called it Treasure Island) opened in February 1939, the creation of fast-talking promoters and the Works Progress Administration. Its theme was "A Pageant of the Pacific" and a panel of architects, headed by the venerable Arthur Brown, Jr. (designer of City Hall), had decreed a style called "Pacific Basin" to match the Exposition's theme.

Treasure Island was a mirror of the architectually exuberant 1930s and the Pacific Basin style was, in the words of Richard Reinhardt, author of *Treasure Island: San Francisco's Exposition Years*, "a unique synchronistic style that had no past and no future." It was a kind of movie-set Shangri-la as Busby Berkeley might have seen it. The highlights were grandly named: the Statue of Pacifica, the Court of the Moon, the Tower of the Sun, and the ninety-foot Arch of Triumph (symbolizing who knew what).

The Second Century

Seventeen million visitors roamed Treasure Island's lavishly landscaped grounds, dropping in to see a scale model of San Francisco in 1999, and, Richard Reinhardt remembered, lavish dioramas of "business and industry, commerce and agriculture, history and science, dioramas of ski slopes, copper mines, college campuses, lumber mills and summer resorts." They sipped coffee at the Brazil Pavilion, or took in one of the innumerable shows: the *Folies Bergére*, Bing Crosby, Benny Goodman, or Billy Rose's *Aquacade* (starring Oakland High graduate Esther Williams). But, Reinhardt writes, "playing Treasure Island was a show business equivalent of ordeal by freezing. The customers were tight with their two-bits; repeaters were rare; and brassy all-girl villages that packed 'em in at Dallas and Cleveland withered and died in San Francisco."

Treasure Island was no match for the Panama-Pacific Exposition twenty-four years earlier. It was too nervously vulgar, too dedicated to making a buck. But, though it ended up losing money in the end, it was glorious fun. Yet a pall hung over its gaiety. Like the Panama-Pacific Exposition, Treasure Island was being stalked by war. Instead of the spanking modern airport the island was to have become after the fair, it became, and still is, a naval base. When it closed in the winter of 1940, it was already a frivolous anachronism. War in Europe had already begun, and in little more than a year the Japanese attacked Pearl Harbor.

Sally Rand's Nude Ranch was an exception, and a sensation. When Treasure Island's art exhibit finally outgrossed the Nude Ranch, the exposition issued a relieved press release. Taste had conquered after all!

World War II: The bombing of Pearl Harbor and the war it started threw the city into forty-six months of frenetic wartime activity that altered it in unexpected ways. As America's major Pacific port, San Francisco was nearly overwhelmed by the needs of the country's war machine. Historian Oscar Lewis has written, "World War II had as great an impact on the city's economy as any event since the Gold Rush almost a century earlier."

Over a million and a half military personnel and twenty-three million tons of war supplies passed through the Golden Gate during the war. The already densely populated city was filled almost to bursting: sailors and soldiers slept in ornate hotel lobbies, restaurants were jammed around the clock, bars were packed with fearful or excited men and women. San Francisco barely kept on the safe side of chaos (and sometimes didn't). Gun emplacements speckled the approaches to the Bay. An antisubmarine net was strung across the Golden Gate, and a few home owners in the Marina, harried by fantasies of the Japanese fleet sailing past their bay windows, sold at a loss and fled. Flummoxed civil defense authorities tried to enforce blackouts, but San Francisco—streaked with deadly earthquake faults, burned and rebuilt more than twice—wasn't a city much inclined to worry about impending disaster.

The war's effect on San Francisco was more than the dramatic comings and goings of troops and tanks. The number of factories in the city increased by a third, and the industrial workforce more than doubled in size. In 1941 there were 101,000 wage earners in the city; by mid-1943 there were 269,000. New shipyards blossomed around the Bay. The sleepy village of Sausalito had nearly 90,000 workers at its Marin shipyards. In San Francisco, the Hunter's Point Naval Shipyard attracted thousands of workers, many of them southern blacks. In 1940 fewer than 5,000 blacks lived in San Francisco. By 1950 their number had grown to 43,000, part of an all-time high city population of 775,357.

When the war ended on VJ Day, August 16, 1945, San Francisco celebrated riotously. Perhaps no city on the mainland had been so intimately affected by the war, and San Francisco, like the rest of the nation, looked forward to peace—and to its own "intensified pursuit of human happiness."

"The City That Waits To Die" has always had a sense of humor about its own precarious existence. Colma, the little cemetery community just south of San Francisco, is nick-named "The City That Waits for the City That Waits to Die to Die."

San Francisco has been losing population for the past thirty years. The 1980 census counted 671,000 San Franciscans.

Today's City

8

One of the surest things to be said about today's San Francisco (and the whole Bay Area) is that since the war it has been at the vanguard of just about every new idea, fad, political movement, crackpot scheme, and earnest effort to cope with the befuddlements of modern times. It has always had a well-bolstered reputation for relishing eccentric notions. No other city in America was built by a horde of gold-grazed young men and their camp followers, people who weren't shy in trying out new ideas, and no other city welcomed every vagabond (he might come up with a new way to make money!) or tolerated most every screwball (he might turn out to be as entertaining as the Emperor Norton, after all).

True, the city has almost always had a flock of settled-down, normal, law-abiding—perhaps even God-fearing—citizens, not always overjoyed at the constant shenanigans. Inevitably, such are the majority of San Franciscans, but there has rarely been a time when the city didn't vibrate a little from the tension between plumb craziness and old-fashioned values. Yet even when those values are being eroded, mocked and ignored, there can't be many San Franciscans who aren't proud of the uniqueness of their city. Not that many haven't been sorely tried by it all. The last three decades have been a headache for nearly everyone, and the proffered remedies have often been rather bizarre. And often concocted in San Francisco.

The Beatnik Begat the . . . : There are many ways to approach today's city, but a good one is through the evolution and mutations of nonconformity and rebelliousness that have begun here and spread across much of the land. During the 1950s, when much of America was

Opposite page
City of experiments: Daring, controversial and very San Francisco, the Transamerica Pyramid rises above the Gold Rush buildings of Jackson Square.

slumbering in prosperity, San Francisco nurtured a movement that in many ways was the first stirring of the fantastic changes the nation was about to undergo. San Francisco novelist Herbert Gold has written of the Beat Movement, "The Beatnik begat the Hippie and the Hippie begat a life style that touches us in ways that extend from fashion and drugs and sexuality to politics and race and a sense of what America might be."

By today's standards, the Beatniks seem rather tame. They weren't really out to destroy society, and their philosophy, if that's the word, really wasn't very threatening; it was more a world-weary contempt for the conventional, for the conformity that seemed to lie so heavily on the land.

In the mid-1950s, San Francisco became an asylum for hundreds of poets, writers, and artists (and those who would be). As much as they gathered around anything, they gathered around the idea of what Jack Kerouac called a "Beat Generation"—beatific, hip, just maybe beat down a little by the lugubriousness of America. Many of the beats settled around North Beach, where they frequented the area's old coffee houses and nursed "dago red" and capuccino long into the night, reading their quirky poetry, and discussing the nature of the universe and the emptiness of modern life. At first no one was much troubled by their mildly shocking ways—"free love," marijuana smoking, and steadfast nonconformity—this was the city of tolerance after all.

But America slowly began to take a titillated interest in the Beatniks. In 1957 Allen Ginsberg wrote his rawly despairing poem "Howl." That same year, Jack Kerouac published *On The Road*, the rambling distillation of the beat pilgrimage. The national news media, for neither the first nor last time, sent emissaries to San Francisco to find out what all the fuss was about, but few reporters had the insight and honesty of a Bayard Taylor or the humor of a Mark Twain. America wasn't able to gather up much sympathy for the delicate angst of the beats. But it could be ruinously curious.

It wasn't long before the beat hangouts—the Café Trieste, poet Lawrence Ferlinghetti's City Lights bookstore, the Co-Existence Bagel Shop—were swamped with tourists, gawkers, and pseudobeatniks. Moral outrage became a cottage industry, and exploiters moved in to sell the beat ethos. The Beatniks themselves gradually took cover, went on new pilgrimages or bought ranch-style houses in the suburbs.

Perhaps they were victims of their own aimlessness, or the withering glare of publicity. More likely though, the beats were done in by the rapid changes rolling across America. The national torpor the beats detested was ending. They were never much for protest anyway, and a contentious time was in the offing.

Herb Caen, San Francisco's columnist laureate, picked up on Jack Kerouac's vague notion and christened the newcomers "beatniks."

Most of the old North Beach coffeehouses are still there, as is the City Lights bookstore. Lawrence Ferlinghetti's poems are occasionally published in, of all places, the *Examiner*; he has become respectable, and the closest thing the city has to a poet laureate. Jack Kerouac died in 1969 but Allen Ginsberg continues to assault the frontiers of human consciousness in his inimitable way.

A Short History of San Francisco

The New Left: In the South, the civil rights movement was gathering strength, offering the country a chance to start a glorious moral crusade. Across the country, the "silent generation" of the 1950s was being replaced by a generation of protest, inspired in part by the Reverend Martin Luther King, Jr., by the nonconformism of the Beatniks, by a gruesome war, and a complex of boredom, affluence, idealism, and youthful energy.

The first great protest of those years took place in San Francisco in 1960. The infamous House Un-American Activities Committee had scheduled a series of meetings in City Hall. Instead of the sympathetic right-wingers it expected, the committee was met in the great rotunda by hundreds of angry protestors. The city's authorities, confronted by placards ("Witch Hunters Go Home") and raised fists and voices, acted as if they had a lunatic riot on their hands. Firehoses were brought into the rotunda and turned on the protestors, police lashed out with billy clubs. In the end, dozens of protestors nursed their wounds and grievances in jail.

A kind of war had been declared. The genius of protest, Abbie Hoffman, remembered, "Two blocks away midday business went on as usual, but in the [rotunda] a generation had cast its spirit into the crucible of resistance." A brushfire of protest spread across the Bay to the University of California's Berkeley campus, which for decades launched missiles of anger and resistance at racism, war, materialism, and economic inequity. From Berkeley the fire spread to the east and to Europe. In time, the Free Speech Movement (first seed of protest at Berkeley) begat the student movement, which begat the New Left, until America's politics, indeed its way of looking at itself, had been profoundly changed.

The Hippies: While the New Left was battling on the political front, another group—as peaceful as the New Left was militant—was emerging in San Francisco. The Hippies hadn't much taste for politics or confrontation; their aims were more charmingly insidious: they meant to change the world through love, kindness, freedom from materialism, and maybe a few drugs to ease the transition.

In many ways, the Hippies picked up where the Beatniks had left off. In fact, many of the old beats slid easily into the Hippie movement: North Beach poet Gregory Corso, Allen Ginsberg, Neal Cassady (hero of *On The Road*), and novelist Ken Kesey, author of *One Flew Over the Cuckoo's Nest* and captain of the famous bus that popped up at nearly every Hippie festival, were among them.

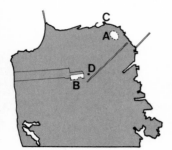

A. North Beach
B. Haight-Ashbury
C. Fisherman's Wharf
D. Author's house

No one is sure where the word hippie originated, and during the mid-1960s, when they began streaming into San Francisco's Haight-Ashbury district, no one was quite sure where they had come from themselves. The Haight was a good neighborhood for the Hippies. Relatively low rents in funky old Victorians suited the ever-shifting communes and crash pads. Haight Street, lined with small shops, had a nice small-town, good-vibes atmosphere, and nearby Golden Gate Park was a handy place to trip out on the creations of God and Uncle John McLaren.

By the late 1960s, the Hippies had virtually taken over the Haight. To recall the Hippies is easy, but it's much more difficult to remember the shock and grumbling and heart-clutching they inspired. Their long hair; scraggly beards; weird, dirty, patchy clothes; childlike trust and promiscuity; casual use of marijuana and LSD were all direct assaults on the values the parent culture held dear. And what was worse was that these bums—to the straights they looked like gypsies or hoboes—actually, knowingly, lovingly *chose* to be bums, turning the success ethic inside out.

In late 1967 the Hippie culture flowered in a huge "Be-In" in Golden Gate Park. The celebrated Summer of Love followed the next year. The Be-In was largely the brainstorm of Allen Ginsberg. It was there that he first experimented with his as yet unsuccessful method of altering earthly consciousness by the mass chanting of the mantra "Om." Typically, the Be-In was an unfocused, unlinear, spontaneous, gloriously ragtag event. To ask what it was for, what it all meant, was to miss the point. It was "an unspoken secret," remembered one Flower Child, a celebration of self (at which San Francisco has always excelled), "a lot of stoned people wandering around blowing their minds on how many others were there. It was like awakening to find you'd been reborn and this was your new family."

For a short time, San Francisco was the world center of a fragile explosion of novelty and undisciplined experiment. The city (and its police) were at first tolerant, even amused. New and challenging (to some tastes, at least) music was being created by the famous bands inspired by the Hippie culture: the Jefferson Airplane, the still active Grateful Dead, and Big Brother and the Holding Company (with lead singer Janis Joplin, a tragic example of Hippie self-indulgence). Eastern religions, with their emphasis on nonattachment and universal love, had infiltrated the Haight, as had (more perniciously) such eager gurus as ex-Harvard scholar Timothy Leary, who blithely preached his drug communion, "Tune in, turn on, drop out."

But it was all sadly ephemeral. Before long the Haight was clogged with tourists, reporters, and pseudohippies. "Hippie" became a world fashion, and like all fashions, it dated. Lost and bewildered children crowded the

Haight, some of them prey for the likes of Charles Manson, who recruited much of his "family" there. The free-floating drugs began to take their toll. Along with tacky head shops and poster stores came rip-off artists and pushers. Marijuana and LSD were replaced by heroin and speed. By the early 1970s, the Haight Ashbury, cosmic capital of Love, was a New Age slum. Love and gentleness had fled.

The Hippies filtered into anonymity. Some have ended up in the suburbs, some sell insurance, some were destroyed by drugs, some still roam the city and the world. But the Hippies, as seasonal as they were, have left their mark. In America, and perhaps especially in San Francisco, the Hippie ethic and radical politics and causes blended together, cross-fertilized, mutated, and created a new way of looking at things. In San Francisco, the home of much of the recent ferment, the result is a city (a region, even a state of mind) that values diversity and toleration, that enjoys and supports innovation, that is always on the track of something new.

After years of false starts, the Haight-Ashbury is just now recovering from its horrible decline after the Hippies left, though reminders of the old days—good and bad—remain.

Into the '80s: In some senses, San Francisco is still a Gold Rush town, still a magnet for the footloose and dissatisfied. Instead of gold, it attracts with beauty, tolerance, and eccentricity. But for every Emperor Norton, for every charming odd-ball, the city has a score of troubled, lost souls.

The intensity of the Bay Area's politics in the 1960s and 1970s created some horrifying caricatures of political activism, like the grotesque Symbionese Liberation Army that kidnapped and brutalized William Randolph Hearst's granddaughter Patricia. It was San Francisco's reputation for tolerance and openness that attracted a bogus minister named Jim Jones to the city. Here, as the world knows, he founded the People's Temple and seduced thousands of people, mostly poor, mostly idealistic, into believing that they could create a halcyon society in the jungles of Guyana.

As America's first great western city, San Francisco has always had its share of violence. From the beginning, much of that violence was generated by the city's restless politics: judges shooting senators and politicians shooting editors. Most of those bloody run-ins had achieved a patina of quaintness over the years, at least until late 1978, when the horror and shock of assassination once more descended on the city. On November 28 that year, a former city supervisor named Dan White assassinated George Moscone, San Francisco's mayor, and Harvey Milk, the city's first homosexual supervisor.

White, a former police and fireman, never testified at his trial, but his motives (on the surface at least) seem clear. Some months before the killings, he had suddenly resigned his seat on the Board of Supervisors. White soon had second thoughts, however, and asked the mayor to reappoint him. At first Moscone agreed, but, under pressure from liberals opposed to the conservative White, the mayor reconsidered. The murders took place on the day he was to appoint a liberal new supervisor to White's old seat. White's motive for killing Harvey Milk is a little less obvious. True, the gay supervisor had been among those advising the mayor not to reappoint White—a reason, if that's the word, for bloody vengeance. But Dan White, a native San Franciscan, a high-school athlete and war veteran, an All-American Boy, was almost surely motivated by a festering anger at the increasing political power of the city's large homosexual population.

On May 22, 1979, White was convicted of voluntary manslaughter. He had pleaded "diminished capacity" on the basis of his (previously unnoticed) mental difficulties. His sentence carried a maximum of seven years in jail. The bizarrely lenient sentence inspired a riot at City Hall when it was announced, incensed gays (and sympathizers) causing $1 million in damages during the so-called White Night Riot.

The City Hall killings and riots pushed San Francisco into a long period of grief and soul-searching. When such things happen, many people feel a sense of guilt, as if the city itself, they themselves, were somehow to blame. The city's new mayor, Mrs. Dianne Feinstein (first elected by her fellow supervisors, and since elected by San Francisco's voters) performed admirably as healer and conciliator for a city confused by itself. But as San Francisco, always self-conscious even in the best of times, inched back to normal, it wondered if it had lost fortune's smile, if the good, old, favored, frivolous and charming San Francisco had disappeared.

Among other things (including pure arbitrariness), the assassinations mirror San Francisco's factious politics. White and Milk had been elected from opposing ends of the political spectrum to represent two of the city's eleven new supervisorial districts. District elections were a reform: after decades of electing city-wide supervisors, the voters had, in 1976, decided to increase the power of the city's new and traditional neighborhoods (and take some power away from the so-called downtown interests that had long dominated the city's political life).

By splitting itself into districts, San Francisco showed that, like many American cities, it had lost some of its sense of unity and consensus. It has always been a city of minorities (in 1970 almost 45 percent of San Franciscans were foreign-born or children of foreign-born parents), and today those groups are less than ever content to follow a paternalistic Establishment.

There are the city's blacks, here as elsewhere victims of racism. There is the rapidly growing Latin population. And there are the gays, a new kind of minority, though none the less militant. The city has almost always had a large number of Orientals, historically rather quiet, now increasingly assertive. It has substantial numbers of Filipinos, Koreans, Samoans, Europeans—even, out on Clement and Geary Streets, an enclave of Russians.

As the saying goes, these minorities are out for a share of the pie. The problem is that San Francisco, like every city in creation, has less and less of a pie to share. The city's tax base is shrinking as it loses population, and as what industry it has moves to the suburbs and the exurbs. The port is a remnant of its former glory, ground down by managerial lassitude and lack of space. The city hasn't escaped the recession of the early 1980s. Jobs are scarce, and the city has begun the inevitable grim cutting of city services and amenities.

Every one of these problems is stalked by a pack of solutions which, consensus having fled, are often bitterly at odds. The old downtown interests, for instance, see a solution for joblessness in new highrises and development. They are opposed by environmentalists who rally against the "Manhattanization" of San Francisco, and by those who think that big business doesn't pay its share of taxes and that most of the office workers in those new highrises live outside the city anyway.

San Francisco's most lucrative industry these days is tourism, to many a mixed blessing. For while almost everyone glories in living in "Everybody's Favorite City," some San Franciscans worry that by selling itself to tourism, the city inevitably sells out—cheapens—the very things the tourists presumably come here to see. So a Fisherman's Wharf, once just that, has become a pastiche of maritime geegaws, dull-witted "museums," fast-food restaurants, and occasionally, a fishing boat. It seems that a difficult thing to do—for very long anyway—is to capture, homogenize, package, and sell "charm."

But then again, that's the kind of thing people have been saying about the city since there were beached sailors and lordly rancheros old enough to remember better days: the relaxed atmosphere of Mexican-America before it was trampled underfoot by the Argonauts; the days before the telegraph ended the city's exquisite isolation, before the railroad barged into town, before this or that war, before the Beatniks, the gays, the Hippies, before—as some old-timers say—the rest of you got here.

And it may be true. The city is always changing, adapting, booming, busting, building and rebuilding. San Francisco hasn't lost its physical beauty. Many marvelous views have been blocked by steel and glass monsters, but it is still, as William Saroyan once write, "a city that invites the heart to come to life . . . an experiment in living."

Experiments: The old New Left-Hippie showboat revolutionary Jerry Rubin not long ago wrote that "The Bay Area seems to give people permission to experiment, to go crazy, try something new. Then the ideas get packaged by the media in New York and are sent as myths to the rest of the country." Rubin himself is a case in point: with the Aquarian Age and the revolution postponed, he came to San Francisco in the 1970s and happily sat down to the smorgasbord of new ideas the city offered. Some of those ideas and experiments are myths and some mere fads. But the longing for newness, the need for it, that fueled the Hippies and the New Left have remained strong enough to make that smorgasbord a full and usually delightful one.

Even San Francisco's politics, as argumentative as they are, offer the hope of a vital experiment. The New Left's emphasis on "people power" is everywhere evident as ethnic, ideological, and sexual groups make their voices heard. And the Hippie ethos of live-and-let-live serves to mediate, to bring tolerance to the debate. As America becomes more multiracial, as more ways of life demand freedom of expression, the country will look to cities like San Francisco for ways to adapt.

Here is where the ecology movement really began, and where it is strongest. Ever since the days when John Muir plugged conservation, San Francisco and the Bay Area have been a world center for the protection of nature, a concern that is increasingly important in a world threatened by an ever-growing number of poisons and ecological disasters.

In 1965 ecology-minded citizens lobbied successfully for the formation of the Bay Conservation and Development Commission, which has done much to control the filling in of the Bay, a frightening 40 percent of which has become land since the innocent days of the Gold Rush. In 1972 California voters, led by San Francisco, created a Coastal Commission that sets strict limitations on development of the state's incomparable coastline. In 1973, at the persistent urging of the Sierra Club, the Golden Gate National Recreation Area was formed. The GGNRA protects San Francisco's Ocean Beach, the Marin Headlands, Angel and Alcatraz Islands, and part of the city's northern waterfront, a magnificent thirty-eight thousand acres of parkland in the midst of a bustling megalopolis. The city is the home of scores of ecology groups, from the powerful Sierra Club, the Friends of the Earth, and the Greenpeace Foundation (which has done so much to save the world's whales from extinction) to local park enthusiasts, backyard gardeners, and alternative energy buffs. And groups like Heritage and the Victorian Alliance are equally active defending San Francisco's man-made ecology from falling victim to the city's historic enemy, greedy developers.

A Short History of San Francisco

San Francisco has always drunk eagerly from the mother's milk of materialism (the Forty-Niners, after all, didn't come for the view), but it has always also had a place for the visionary and the otherworldly. Today the city is a center for every kind of spiritual quest: "mainline" churches, Zen monasteries, storefront missions, witch covens, swami-led communes, and odd sects of three or two or one, all the way up to huge semicults like Erhard Seminars Training (*est*).

However moonstruck some of these groups seem (and are!) they are symptoms of a spiritual crisis in American life, and somewhere in that hodgepodge are important ethical and religious lessons waiting to be disseminated. The same stockbroker or taxi-driver who keeps up on the latest meditation techniques is also likely to watch his or her diet, exercise regularly, all the things that the "holistic health" movement, very prominent in the city, espouses. Despite its hills, San Francisco and the Bay Area are teeming with runners.

San Francisco has never been compared with, say, New York, as an artistic capital, though it has nurtured and produced a surprising number of geniuses, near-geniuses and amusing charlatans. In its early years it proudly domiciled Mark Twain, Bret Harte, and a legion of poets, painters, and writers slightly less accomplished but not a bit less taken with the city's uniqueness. At the turn of the century, the city's literati included the superb realist novelist Frank Norris, the incomparable Jack London, and the popular devotee of Old California, Gertrude Atherton. Later in the century, the likes of Dashiell Hammett, William Saroyan, and Henry Miller moved in and out of the city, taking part in its artistic ferment. Today's city is justifiably proud of its writers and poets.

Always a great theater town, San Francisco today boasts one of America's finest provincial acting companies, the American Conservatory Theater, along with a healthy number of experimental and neighborhood groups. The city has also lately become the spiritual home of an influential group of young filmmakers like Francis Ford Coppola, Gary Kurtz, and Steven Spielberg.

But San Francisco's artistic contribution probably lies in its style of doing things rather than in a high-priced finished product. The patroness of the city's creators might be Isadora Duncan, a local girl whose dances are lost to us, but whose relentless and courageous experimentation is still inspiring. The arts in San Francisco are notably unstuffy and freewheeling. They are products of a long tradition of experimentation, very much a part of the ethic so prevalent in this city: democratization, participation, innovation, sharing, having fun.

The marvelously eccentric Vedanta Temple—a good example of San Francisco's otherworldly side—was built in 1905 at the corner of Webster and Filbert streets by a benign sect founded in 1900 by Swami Trigunatitananda.

The Heart Comes to Life: As much as San Francisco can claim to be the home of trends and ideas, as many of its citizens are earnestly engaged in trying out new techniques to survive and enjoy an uncertain future, the city's real charm springs from its ability, as Saroyan, a real life-embracer and hell-raiser, said "to invite the heart to come to life."

And it has always been that way: the Ohlone gloried in the Bay's fecundity and beauty, the Spanish padres blessed its loveliness, and the Forty-Niners arrived bursting with youthful vitality and built a city that mirrored their passion for life.

It has always been a city that exalted the senses—a city of fine restaurants, raucous taverns, elegant mansions, and exciting music; a city of proud, high-stepping men and women, a city that changes by the moment, each moment offering a new inspiration, a new view.

Always a city of views: from atop Twin Peaks, the city can appear a glistening jewel or a mysterious "cool grey city of love," as George Sterling called it; from Fillmore and Broadway, a sudden vision of the Golden Gate Bridge, the Mediterranean colors of the marina, the green hills of Marin, the Palace of Fine Arts; looking down California Street from a cable car, past Chinatown's pagodalike buildings, past the scurrying traffic and august structures of the Wall Street of the West, down to the blue of the Bay.

Always a city of colors and sudden delights: the bustling street life of the Mission; of Castro Street on a sunny day; the little bit of Tokyo in one of Japantown's sushi bars; the exotic dailiness of Chinatown's traditional markets; the street mimes and artists; the cooling fog and seawashed air.

Always a city of the unexpected, from Gold Rushes and earthquakes to tragedy and style and experimentation, never quite the same, always San Francisco.

Selected Bibliography

Caughey, John Walton. *The California Gold Rush*. Berkeley and Los Angeles: University of California Press, 1975.

Hansen, Gladys. *San Francisco Almanac: Everything You Want To Know about The City*. San Francisco: Chronicle Books, 1975. Thousands of facts and figures, not a single one of them trivial.

Hinckle, Warren. *The Richest Place on Earth*. Boston: Houghton Mifflin Co., 1978. A modern writer's rococo account of the Comstock silver mines.

Lewis, Oscar. *Sketches of Early California*. San Francisco: Chronicle Books, 1971.

Lockwood, Charles. *Suddenly San Francisco*. San Francisco: California Living Books, 1978. Ends with the 1906 earthquake.

McGloin, Father John, S.J. *San Francisco: The Story of a City*. San Rafael, Calif.: Presidio Press, 1978.

Margolin, Malcolm. *The Ohlone Way*. Berkeley: Heyday Books, 1978. A moving evocation of the Bay Area's earliest settlers.

Muscatine, Doris. *Old San Francisco: The Biography of a City, from Early Days to the Earthquake*. New York: G. P. Putnam's Sons, 1975. A dense but readable history.

Reinhardt, Richard. *Treasure Island: San Francisco's Exposition Years*. San Francisco: Scrimshaw Press, 1973.

Royce, Josiah. *California: A Study of American Character*. 1886. Reprint. New York: Alfred A. Knopf, 1948. An early, entertaining revisionist history of the state's not so heroic beginnings.

Starr, Kevin. *Americans and the California Dream, 1850–1915*. New York: Oxford University Press, 1973. An interpretation of California's (and San Francisco's) magnetic allure, written in an erudite, calmly witty style.

Taylor, Bayard. *Eldorado; or Adventures in the Path of Empire*. 1850. Reprint. New York: Alfred A. Knopf, 1949. The classically intrepid reporter covering one of history's greatest stories.

Twain, Mark. *Roughing It*. 1871. Reprint. Berkeley and Los Angeles: University of California Press, 1972. Twain's genius nurtured in the money-mad Comstock Lode; superb fun.

Walker, Franklin A. *San Francisco's Literary Frontier*. 1939. Reprint. Seattle: University of Washington Press, 1970.

Watkins, T. H., and Olmsted, R. R. *Here Today*. San Francisco: Chronicle Books, 1968. A good account of the city's architectural heritage; a present to the city from San Francisco's Junior League.

———. *Mirror of the Dream*. San Francisco: Scrimshaw Press, 1976. Witty, opinionated, beautifully illustrated, and increasingly hard to find.

Herewith is an entirely personal list of books the author found particularly fascinating and informative. The confirmed San Franciscophile will have his or her own list, and those new to the literature should have no problem finding books on every nuance of the city, from its knifemakers to its madams.

Index